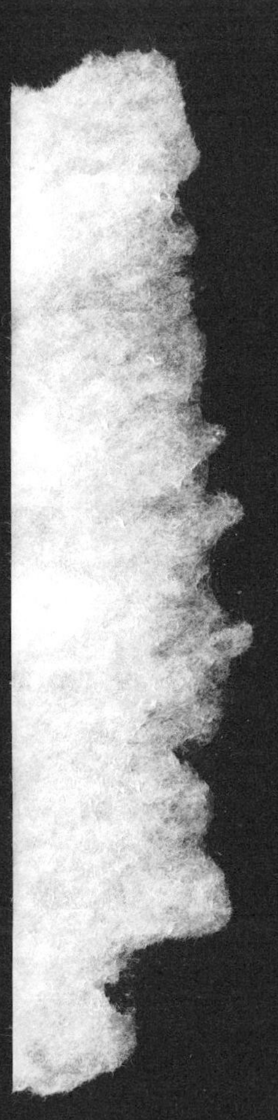

# Spink's
# Catalogue of British and associated Orders, Decorations and Medals
*with valuations*

# *Spink's*

# Catalogue of British and associated Orders, Decorations and Medals

*with valuations*

E. C. JOSLIN

*To my wife Peggy who has patiently allowed me to 'meddle' for almost four decades.*



First published in Great Britain 1983 by
Webb & Bower (Publishers) Limited
9 Colleton Crescent, Exeter, Devon EX2 4BY
in association with Limelight Limited
15 Castle Street, Exeter

Designed by Vic Giolitto



**British Library Cataloguing in Publication Data**
Joslin, E.C.
Spink's catalogue of British and
associated orders, decorations and medals.
1. Decorations of honour—Great Britain—
collections and collecting
I. Title
737'.2 CR4871
ISBN 0-906671-68-X



Typeset in Great Britain by Keyspools Limited
Golborne, Warrington WA3 3QA

Printed and bound in Hong Kong by Mandarin Offset
International Limited

# Contents

# Collecting

Many collectors are familiar with the earlier Standard Catalogues which were first pioneered by Spink & Son Ltd in 1969. However, it has been apparent for some time that the collector now requires a more detailed and sophisticated price structure, considerably wider in scope and superior than all previous publications.

Nevertheless, in preparing this work, the author has taken into account the need to introduce this fascinating collecting series to the general public and satisfy those who have a family medal or medals in their possession which need identifying and valuing. It is hoped that this publication will, therefore, satisfy the needs of the general public, the new collector and the experienced collector.

The collecting of medals as a hobby has been practised for over a hundred years, but it is only in the last thirty-five years that we have seen an increased activity in this field. The series of orders, decorations and medals, particularly the British series (the issue of which has always been restricted to the actual recipients), represents our Island's proud heritage of naval, military and air achievements during the last two hundred years. The possession of these awards helps to recall a particular war, campaign or action and helps to keep alive the services of a particular officer, man or regiment or perhaps some outstanding act of gallantry. With our diminishing armed forces, these medals serve as a constant reminder of the outstanding and yet often forgotten deeds of our ancestors, such as:

1. Nelson's defeat of the French at the Battle of the Nile, thus saving Egypt and, indirectly, India from French conquest.
2. Nelson's overwhelming defeat of the combined French and Spanish fleets at Trafalgar which finally ruled out Napoleon's invasion plans for these islands.
3. The masterly retreat and evacuation at Corunna in 1809 under the leadership of General Sir John Moore.
4. Wellington's brilliant campaigns against the previously all-victorious French Army in Spain and Portugal from 1809–14.
5. The charge of the Light Brigade at Balaklava.
6. The heroic defence of Rorke's Drift, 1879, by 139 men, when surrounded by an overwhelming force of about 3000 Zulu warriors.
7. The retreat from Mons by the 'Contemptible Little Army' in the face of overwhelming German superiority.
8. The Falkland Islands episode—and countless others.

Such is the wealth of material available covering outstanding events in our history that the collector, whether he be an established one or one who has recently taken up the hobby, is in need of a price catalogue such as those that can be found for stamps, coins and other collecting fields.

The first collectors were few and far between, being mostly wealthy people. Many built large collections which would be impossible to form today, partly due to current price structure, but mainly because the wealth of material at that time seldom becomes available today. The collectors of that era often dealt with their own favourite dealer and these again were few and far between. Today there are far more collectors representing a remarkable cross-section of the community, both in this country and abroad. The collecting of British orders, decorations and medals is becoming an even more popular movement in countries such as Australia, Canada, New Zealand, the USA and the countries where British communities are to be found, such as the Arabian Gulf.

## What to Collect

The range of British orders, decorations and medals is very considerable. Therefore, right at the very outset, one should give considerable thought as to what to collect so as to obtain maximum enjoyment and satisfaction from the hobby. There is a very wide basis for the formation of a collection and one probably cannot go far wrong by choosing one or a combination of the following as a basis:

1. By name: it follows that if one's family name is reasonably common, then one could collect to 'the clan'. However, if one's family name is unusual, then one would be rather frustrated from the very beginning.
2. One could collect one of each type or variety, irrespective of whether they be (a) **Orders**, and here there is a very wide range if one includes all classes and all types, as well as military *and* civil divisions—possibly a fairly expensive and lengthy undertaking, but there is of course plenty of scope. (b) **Decorations for gallantry**, and here one might at the beginning restrict the collection to those issued to the Navy or the Army, or perhaps the Royal Air Force, or the Commonwealth. (c) **Campaign medals**, to collect one of each type is perhaps a fairly reasonable undertaking, provided one does not expect to obtain every different bar that was issued. Here the scope could be restricted by collecting to one regiment, perhaps one's county regiment or to a unit that one or one's family had served in or been associated with. Campaign medals might be collected by period, restricted, say, to the Victorian era, or perhaps those issued during this century, or one might choose the Napoleonic period. The latter has the advantage that they are well documented, but the medals are fairly expensive. The later Victorian campaign medals give one more scope from the price point of view, the Boer War medals starting at £20 to £30 each. Another basis might be to collect medals for just one war and really specialize, and here again, of course, the Boer War or indeed the First World War gives one ample scope, and there is the advantage with these two wars that the price structure is much more reasonable. One might collect by area, for example the Indian subcontinent or medals issued for and around Africa. (d) **Long service medals** could be a study in themselves and of late several very interesting and informative booklets by Major J. M. A. Tamplin, published by Spink & Son Ltd, have been produced which can only add to interest and indeed prices in years to come. The range of long service medals and the various types awarded are quite considerable, and price structure is reasonable when considering the numbers awarded or, in certain cases the few which have survived today, which is perhaps more important. (e) **Jubilee and Coronation medals** are a series that can provide an interesting theme, but here, of course, the majority were issued unnamed, so one does not have the enjoyment of research.

## General Review of Values

While coin collecting goes back as far as nearly two thousand years, war-medal collecting basically resulted from the issue of the first medal awarded to officers and other ranks alike, which was officially named, ie Waterloo

1815. The British medal series is almost unique, or at least most unusual, in that medals have always been severely restricted to those who had participated in an action, and could not be freely purchased across the counter so to speak. This aspect immediately places a scarcity value on orders, decorations and medals. Futhermore, remarkably few of the earlier medals, and indeed some of the medals of this century, have survived, in fact it has been proved that less than five per cent of the earlier Victorian issues exists today. Many, of course, have been lost, many retained by families, which naturally will never come on to the market, while many, during the years of depression particularly in the 1920s and '30s, were melted down because of their bullion value.

After a period covering the last twenty years, when prices constantly rose, often quite dramatically, 1982 saw prices 'peaking out' and then falling by an average of some fifteen per cent. However, by the end of 1982, prices 'bottomed out' and values are once again increasing. In fact, it is interesting to note that this series has probably stood up to the economic ravages of recent times better than any other, which illustrates the remarkable strength of the hobby.

But what of the future? It is felt that the economy will not become any more depressed and we may see an upturn very soon. This, coupled with an ever decreasing supply of most awards and increased demand, must mean price stability or, more likely, price increases.

## Points to bear in mind with regard to valuations

When studying the price structure of the various awards *always* bear in mind the following points:

1. *Condition*
   Throughout the whole series, prices have been based on awards in Very Fine to Extremely Fine (VF/EF) condition.

2. *Orders*
   Prices against all of the orders of chivalry are based on standard government issues. Values of privately made examples of the returnable orders, such as the Order of the Garter, etc, depend on age and also the quality of manufacture.

3. *Gallantry awards*
   Most of the prices for gallantry awards have been based on those for periods, areas or campaigns which earned the majority of awards. Furthermore, prices are based on general citations where appropriate, ie, where no detail of the act of gallantry appears in the *London Gazette*. I cannot emphasize too strongly that the act itself and the theatre of war play a very important part in assessing market values of gallantry awards. For instance, a Second World War V.C. would normally be of more value than a Crimea or Indian Mutiny award, both of which were often issued for lesser acts of valour than later awards. In addition, a larger number were frequently awarded for the earlier campaigns in proportion to the number of troops present. A Distinguished Service Medal for the First World War, awarded for distinguished service over a period of six months, would not be so desirable as one issued for a particular act of gallantry at, say, the Battle of Jutland. Awards that cannot be attributed or unnamed awards are of course not so attractive to the collector. When awards are complete with biographical details, certificates or log books, etc, they usually have a higher price structure.

4. *Campaign medals*
All campaign medals have been assessed on the assumption that they have been awarded to seamen, private soldiers or airmen. If awarded to more senior ranks, then it would be fair to add the undermentioned minimum percentages:

1. NCOs *above* the rank of corporal, +20%
2. Junior officers up to and including captain, +40%
3. Major and Lt-Col, +70%
4. Colonels and above, +100%

Throughout the campaign medal series, the basis for price structure is medals awarded to the largest unit. Cases where just a small number of 'odd' men were present from a regiment or ship have had to be ignored.

5. *Numbers issued*
Where this is known with reasonable accuracy, the number is mentioned in the text or is contained in brackets before the price, however, it cannot be emphasized too strongly that it is also the number that appear in the market that also influences the price structure. The author's intimate knowledge and day to day dealing over almost four decades places him in an unrivalled position to ascertain demand and provide valuations.

6. *Multiple-bar medals*
While it is logical to assume that one simply checks the value of each bar and then adds them up, price structure, unfortunately, does not always follow logic. What one has to do in the case of, say, a multiple Naval General Service Medal is to assess the value of the rarest bar and then add about a quarter of the single bar value of the other bars present. At the present time, it is not often that the different combinations of bars on a medal have any appreciable effect on prices, unless they are rather exceptional.

7. *Groups*
Many years or even decades ago, we often sold a group of medals for less than the total value of the individually priced medals, simply to encourage collectors to keep the group together. Today, the pendulum has swung the other way, and the tendency now is to add a premium which cannot be accurately defined as so much depends on the biographical and/or service record of the recipient. Another aspect which increases the premium for a group is the inclusion of long service awards and unusual combinations.

8. *Prices*
All prices quoted are intended to be in line with those charged or expected to be charged by the average specialized dealer.

9. *Rare Medals/Bars*
Due to the ever decreasing supply of many medals compared to the ever increasing number of collectors throughout most parts of the world, some medals or bars seldom appear on the market and, in these cases, a comparison has been made with similar scarce medals that have been on the market *plus* an assessment based on the author's intimate knowledge regarding the likely demand—a very important aspect.

10 *Renamed Medals*
Officially named medals are collected because they can immediately be identified with the actual recipient—records are frequently available

which makes it possible to trace the military service record of the recipient. It follows, therefore, that if the medal has been renamed, a very considerable proportion of the value has been destroyed. In fact, in years gone by, it was the habit of dealers to frequently melt and scrap medals that had been renamed or tampered with, but today, because of higher values of medals, one does see medals advertised as 're-named'. In these cases, it would be best to ignore them, but if one simply cannot afford to buy an originally named medal because of its high price structure, then of course, a renamed medal would fill a gap in one's collection. For such a purpose, one might consider paying perhaps 15–20% of the value as if it were a correctly named medal.

The term 'renamed' implies that the original naming has been removed and reimpressed or re-engraved with a new rank and name, etc. This renaming was often carried out because a medal contained errors of rank or spelling. Sometimes, original medals were lost, and the recipient then purchased a similar medal from a local source, removed the original naming and re-engraved it.

11 *Conditions*

While it must be readily admitted that condition is not so important as with coin collecting, condition does have some effect on price structure and, generally speaking, collectors should be encouraged where possible to buy a medal in the best possible condition. When the time comes to selling the collection or exchanging a medal, the items in VF/EF condition or better will always be more saleable and will probably fetch a premium.

The undermentioned abbreviations are those normally used to describe conditions:

FDC—Fleur de Coin (faultless or mint condition)
EF—Extremely Fine
VF—Very Fine
F—Fine
Worn.

If a medal falls between the above categories, a combination is frequently used, such as VF/EF. It is suggested that a collector should try and avoid any medal in less than VF condition unless it is extremely rare

12. *Research*

Any research available regarding recipients does have some bearing on values, but not perhaps quite as much as one might think. It is often the actual research which frequently gives many collectors great enjoyment; consequently, a proportion of them are somewhat reluctant to pay other people to spoil this enjoyment! However, specialist researchers are now offering their services and I recommend the under-mentioned who are frequently able to extract considerable information from the Government archives, the fee charged depending of course on the amount of work involved.

Judith Farrington, BA(Hons)
73 Linkfield Road
Isleworth
Middlesex TW7 6QP
Telephone: 01-560 5478

Diana Birch, MA
Diana Birch Research Services
90 Dartmouth Road
Forest Hill
London SE23
Telephone: 01-699 0914

13. *Finally*, remember that the price structure is only a guide as every medal is an individual.

# The order of wearing Orders, Decorations and Medals

Victoria Cross (V.C.)
George Cross (G.C.)
Order of the Garter (K.G.)
Order of the Thistle (K.T.)
Order of St. Patrick (K.P.)
Order of the Bath (G.C.B., K.C.B. and D.C.B., and C.B.)
Order of Merit (O.M.; ranks next after G.C.B.)
Order of the Star of India (G.C.S.I., K.C.S.I. and C.S.I.)
Order of St. Michael and St. George (G.C.M.G., K.C.M.G. and D.C.M.G., and C.M.G.)
Order of the Indian Empire (G.C.I.E., K.C.I.E. and C.I.E.)
Order of the Crown of India (C.I.)
Royal Victorian Order (G.C.V.O., K.C.V.O. and D.C.V.O., and C.V.O.)
Order of the British Empire (G.B.E., K.B.E. and D.B.E., and C.B.E.)
Order of the Companions of Honour (C.H.; ranks next after G.B.E.)
Distinguished Service Order (D.S.O.)
Royal Victorian Order (M.V.O.; Class IV)
Order of the British Empire (O.B.E.)
Queen's Service Order (Q.S.O.)
Imperial Service Order (I.S.O.)
Royal Victorian Order (M.V.O.; Class V)
Order of the British Empire (M.B.E.)
Indian Order of Merit (Military)3Order of Burma (for gallantry) (O.B.)
Royal Red Cross (Class I; R.R.C.)
Distinguished (formerly Conspicuous) Service Cross (D.S.C.)
Military Cross (M.C.)
Distinguished Flying Cross (D.F.C.)
Air Force Cross (A.F.C.)
Royal Red Cross (Class II; A.R.R.C.)
Order of British India (O.B.I.)
Kaisar-i-Hind Medal
Order of Burma (for good service) (O.B.)
Order of St. John
Albert Medal (A.M.)
Union of South Africa King's (Queen's) Medal for Bravery, in gold
Distinguished Conduct Medal (D.C.M.)
Conspicuous Gallantry Medal (C.G.M.)
George Medal (G.M.)
King's (Queen's) Police Medal, for Gallantry (K.P.M., K.P.F.S.M., Q.P.M.)
Queen's Fire Service Medal, for Gallantry (Q.F.S.M.)
Edward Medal (E.M.)
Royal West African Frontier Force Distinguished Conduct Medal (D.C.M.)
King's African Rifles Distinguished Conduct Medal (D.C.M.)
Indian Distinguished Service Medal (I.D.S.M.)
Burma Gallantry Medal (B.G.M.)

Union of South Africa King's (Queen's) Medal for Bravery, in silver
Distinguished Service Medal (D.S.M.)
Military Medal (M.M.)
Distinguished Flying Medal (D.F.M.)
Air Force Medal (A.F.M.)
Constabulary Medal (Ireland)
Board of Trade Medal for Saving Life at Sea (S.G.M.)
Indian Order of Merit (Civil) (I.O.M.)
Empire Gallantry Medal (E.G.M.)
Indian Police Medal for Gallantry
Burma Police Medal for Gallantry
Ceylon Police Medal for Gallantry
Sierra Leone Police Medal for Gallantry
Sierra Leone Fire Brigade Medal for Gallantry
Colonial Police Medal for Gallantry
Queen's Gallantry Medal (Q.G.M.)
Queen's Service Medal (Q.S.M.)
Uganda Services Medal (if awarded for gallantry)
British Empire Medal (B.E.M.)
Canada Medal (C.M. or M. du C.)
Life Saving Medal of the Order of St. John
King's (Queen's) Police Medal for Distinguished Service (K.P.M., K.P.F.S.M., Q.P.M.)
Queen's Fire Service Medal for Distinguished Service (Q.F.S.M.)
Queen's Medal for Chiefs
War Medals (in order of date of campaign)
Polar Medals (in order of date)
Royal Victorian Medal (in gold, silver or bronze)
Imperial Service Medal
Police Medals for Meritorious Service
Uganda Services Medal (if awarded for meritorious service)
Badge of Honour
Jubilee, Coronation and Durbar Medals
King George V Long and Faithful Service Medal
King George VI Long and Faithful Service Medal
Queen Elizabeth II Long and Faithful Service Medal
Efficiency and Long Service Decorations and Medals, Medals for Champion Shots, Independence, etc., Medals
Other Comionwealth Orders, Decorations and Medals (instituted since 1949, otherwise than by the Sovereign) and awards by the States of Malaysia and the State of Brunei
Foreign Orders (in order of date of award)
Foreign Decorations (in order of date of award)
Foreign Medals (in order of date of award)

# Ribands

**Widths of Ribands used with Insignia and on Riband Bars**

| | *with Insignia* | *on Uniform* |
|---|---|---|
| K.G. | 4″ | not worn |
| K.T. | 4″ | not worn |
| K.P. | 4″ | not worn |
| G.C.B. | 4″ | $1\frac{1}{2}$″ |
| G.C.B. (Dame Grand Cross) | $2\frac{1}{4}$″ | $1\frac{1}{2}$″ |
| K.C.B. | 2″ | $1\frac{1}{2}$″ |
| D.C.B. | $1\frac{3}{4}$″ | $1\frac{1}{2}$″ |
| C.B. | $1\frac{1}{2}$″ | $1\frac{1}{2}$″ |
| O.M. | 2″ | 2″ |
| G.C.S.I. | 4″ | $1\frac{1}{2}$″ |
| K.C.S.I. | 2″ | $1\frac{1}{2}$″ |
| C.S.I. | $1\frac{1}{2}$″ | $1\frac{1}{2}$″ |
| G.C.M.G. | 4″ | $1\frac{1}{2}$″ |
| G.C.M.G. (Dame Grand Cross) | $2\frac{1}{4}$″ | $1\frac{1}{2}$″ |
| K.C.M.G. | 2″ | $1\frac{1}{2}$″ |
| D.C.M.G. | $1\frac{3}{4}$″ | $1\frac{1}{2}$″ |
| C.M.G. | $1\frac{1}{2}$″ | $1\frac{1}{2}$″ |
| G.C.I.E. | 4″ | $1\frac{1}{2}$″ |
| K.C.I.E. | 2″ | $1\frac{1}{2}$″ |
| C.I.E. | $1\frac{1}{2}$″ | $1\frac{1}{2}$″ |
| G.C.V.O. | $3\frac{3}{4}$″ | $1\frac{1}{4}$″ |
| D.G.C.V.O. | $2\frac{1}{4}$″ | $1\frac{1}{4}$″ |
| K.C.V.O. | $1\frac{3}{4}$″ | $1\frac{1}{4}$″ |
| D.C.V.O. | $1\frac{3}{4}$″ | $1\frac{1}{4}$″ |
| C.V.O. | $1\frac{3}{4}$″ | $1\frac{1}{4}$″ |
| M.V.O. (4th cl) | $1\frac{1}{4}$″ | $1\frac{1}{4}$″ |
| M.V.O. (5th cl) | $1\frac{1}{4}$″ | $1\frac{1}{4}$″ |
| Royal Victorian Medal | $1\frac{1}{4}$″ | $1\frac{1}{4}$″ |
| G.B.E. | 4″ | $1\frac{1}{2}$″ |
| D.G.C.B.E. | $2\frac{1}{4}$″ | $1\frac{1}{2}$″ |
| K.B.E. | $1\frac{3}{4}$″ | $1\frac{1}{2}$″ |
| D.B.E. | $1\frac{3}{4}$″ | $1\frac{1}{2}$″ |
| C.B.E. | $1\frac{3}{4}$″ | $1\frac{1}{2}$″ |
| O.B.E. | $1\frac{1}{2}$″ | $1\frac{1}{2}$″ |
| M.B.E. | $1\frac{1}{2}$″ | $1\frac{1}{2}$″ |
| B.E.M. | $1\frac{1}{4}$″ | $1\frac{1}{4}$″ |
| C.H. | $1\frac{1}{2}$″ | $1\frac{1}{2}$″ |
| D.S.O. | $1\frac{1}{8}$″ | $1\frac{1}{8}$″ |
| C.I. | $1\frac{1}{2}$″ | $1\frac{1}{2}$″ |
| **Order of St. John** | | |
| Baliff Grand Cross | 4″ | $1\frac{1}{2}$″ |
| Dame Grand Cross | $2\frac{1}{4}$″ | $1\frac{1}{2}$″ |
| Knight of Justice | 2″ | $1\frac{1}{2}$″ |
| Dame of Justice | $1\frac{1}{4}$″ | $1\frac{1}{4}$″ |
| Knight of Grace | 2″ | $1\frac{1}{2}$″ |
| Dame of Grace | $1\frac{1}{4}$″ | $1\frac{1}{4}$″ |
| Chaplain | 2″ | $1\frac{1}{2}$″ |
| Commander (Brother) | $1\frac{1}{2}$″ | $1\frac{1}{2}$″ |
| Commander (Sister) | $1\frac{1}{4}$″ | $1\frac{1}{4}$″ |
| Officer (Brother) | $1\frac{1}{2}$″ | $1\frac{1}{2}$″ |
| Officer (Sister) | $1\frac{1}{4}$″ | $1\frac{1}{4}$″ |
| Serving Brother | $1\frac{1}{2}$″ | $1\frac{1}{2}$″ |
| Serving Sister | $1\frac{1}{4}$″ | $1\frac{1}{4}$″ |

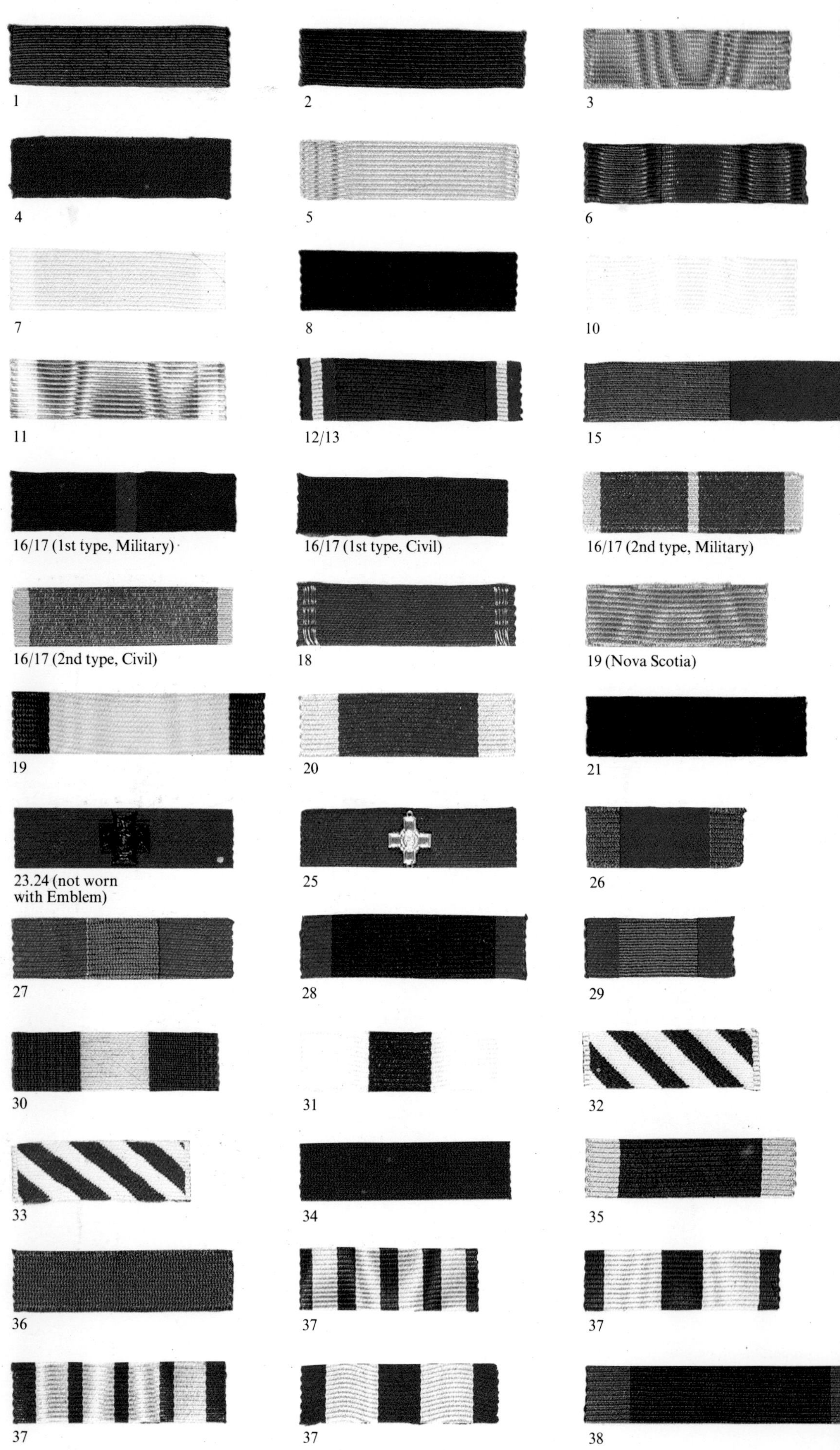
1
2
3
4
5
6
7
8
10
11
12/13
15
16/17 (1st type, Military)
16/17 (1st type, Civil)
16/17 (2nd type, Military)
16/17 (2nd type, Civil)
18
19 (Nova Scotia)
19
20
21
23.24 (not worn with Emblem)
25
26
27
28
29
30
31
32
33
34
35
36
37
37
37
37
38

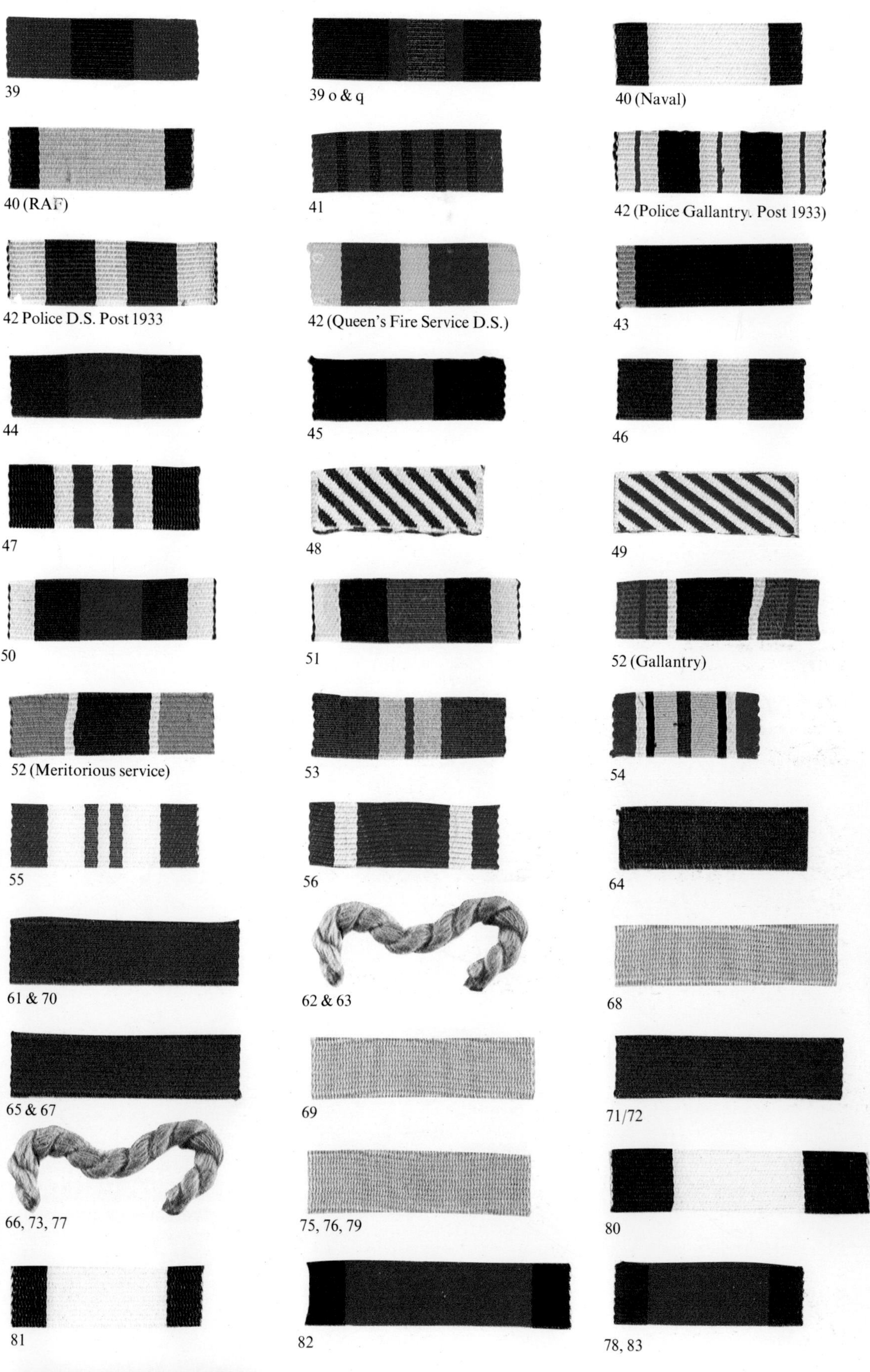
39
39 o & q
40 (Naval)
40 (RAF)
41
42 (Police Gallantry. Post 1933)
42 Police D.S. Post 1933
42 (Queen's Fire Service D.S.)
43
44
45
46
47
48
49
50
51
52 (Gallantry)
52 (Meritorious service)
53
54
55
56
64
61 & 70
62 & 63
68
65 & 67
69
71/72
66, 73, 77
75, 76, 79
80
81
82
78, 83
84

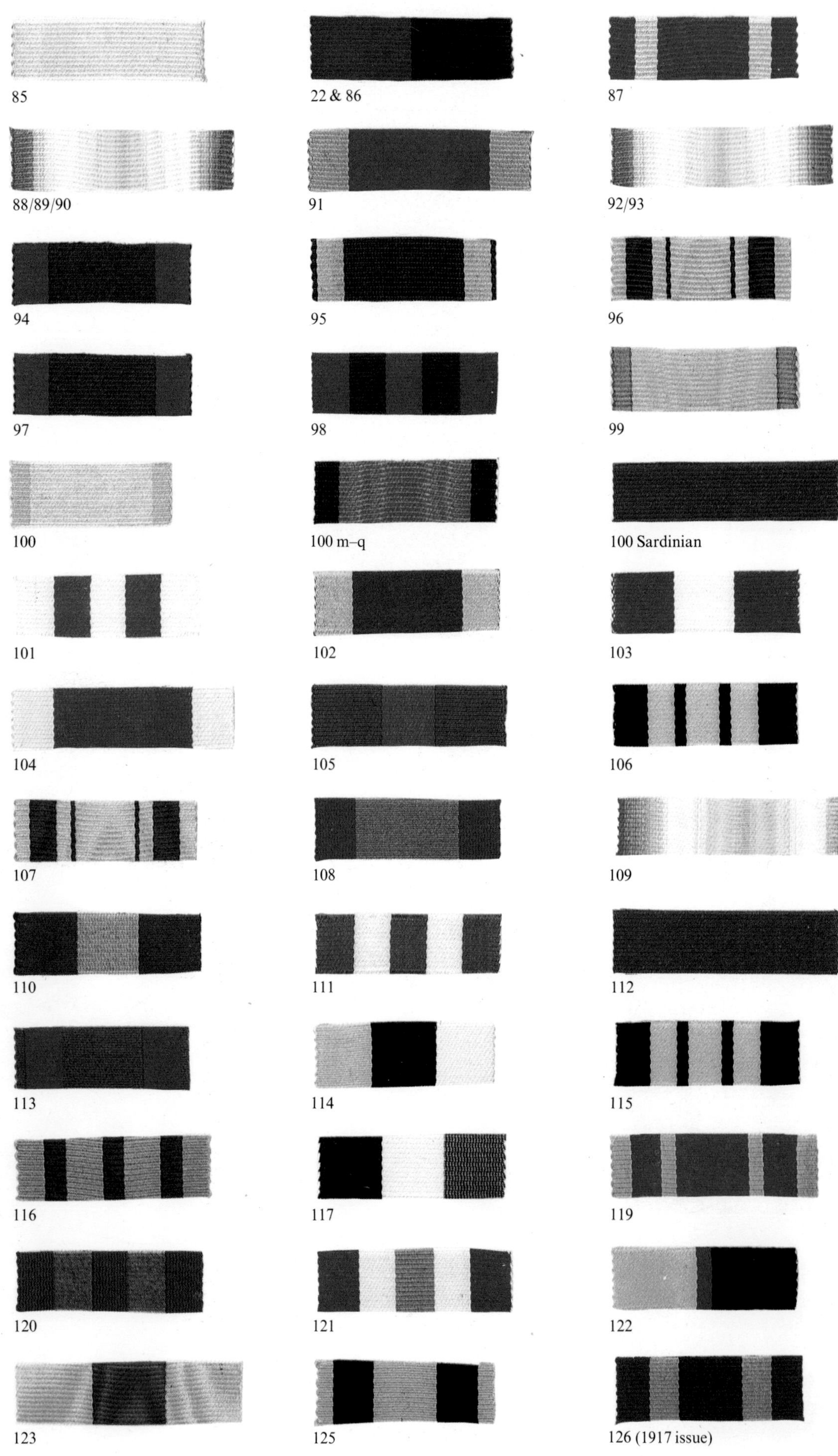
85
22 & 86
87
88/89/90
91
92/93
94
95
96
97
98
99
100
100 m–q
100 Sardinian
101
102
103
104
105
106
107
108
109
110
111
112
113
114
115
116
117
119
120
121
122
123
125
126 (1917 issue)

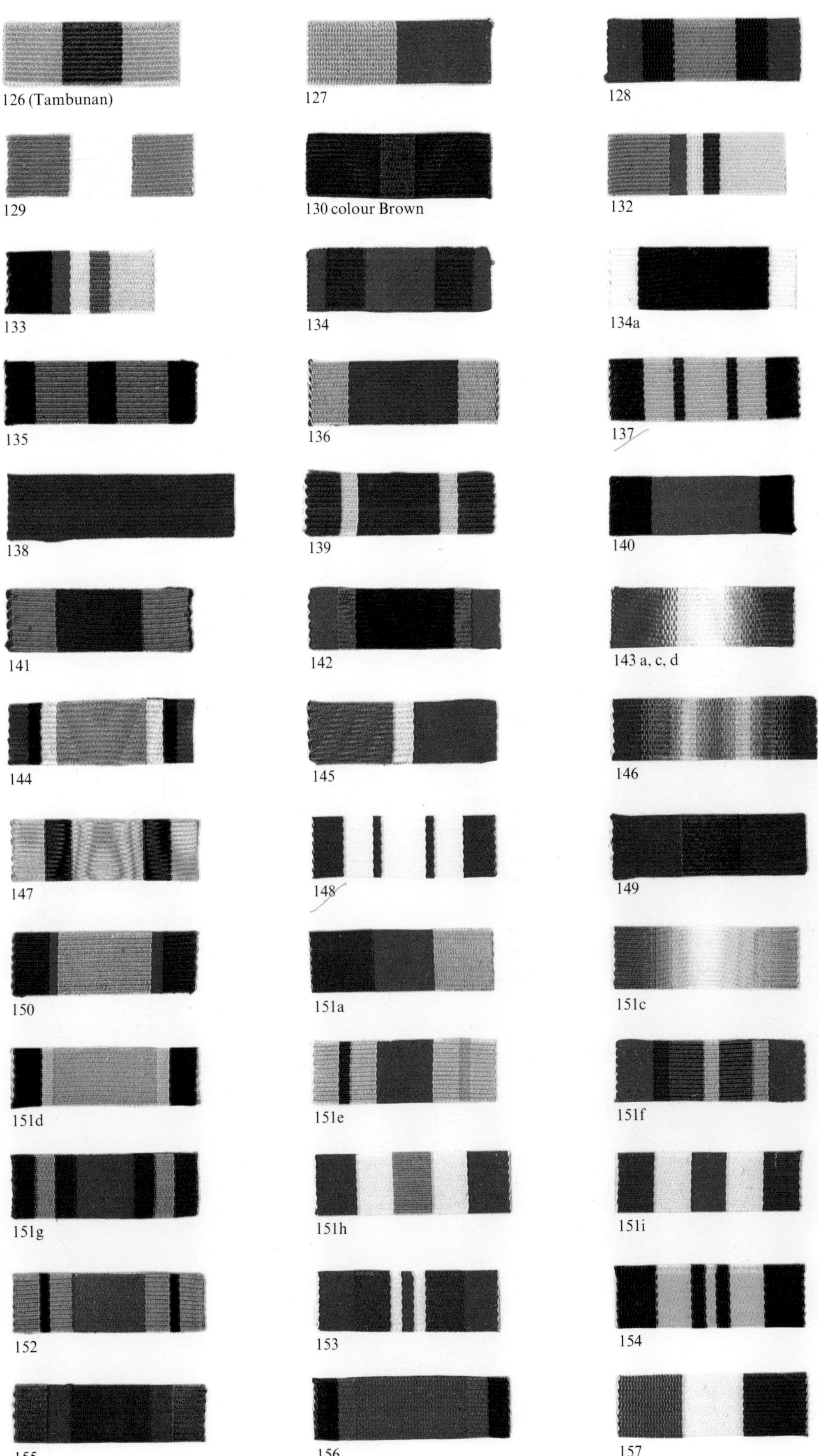
126 (Tambunan)
127
128
129
130 colour Brown
132
133
134
134a
135
136
137
138
139
140
141
142
143 a, c, d
144
145
146
147
148
149
150
151a
151c
151d
151e
151f
151g
151h
151i
152
153
154
155
156
157

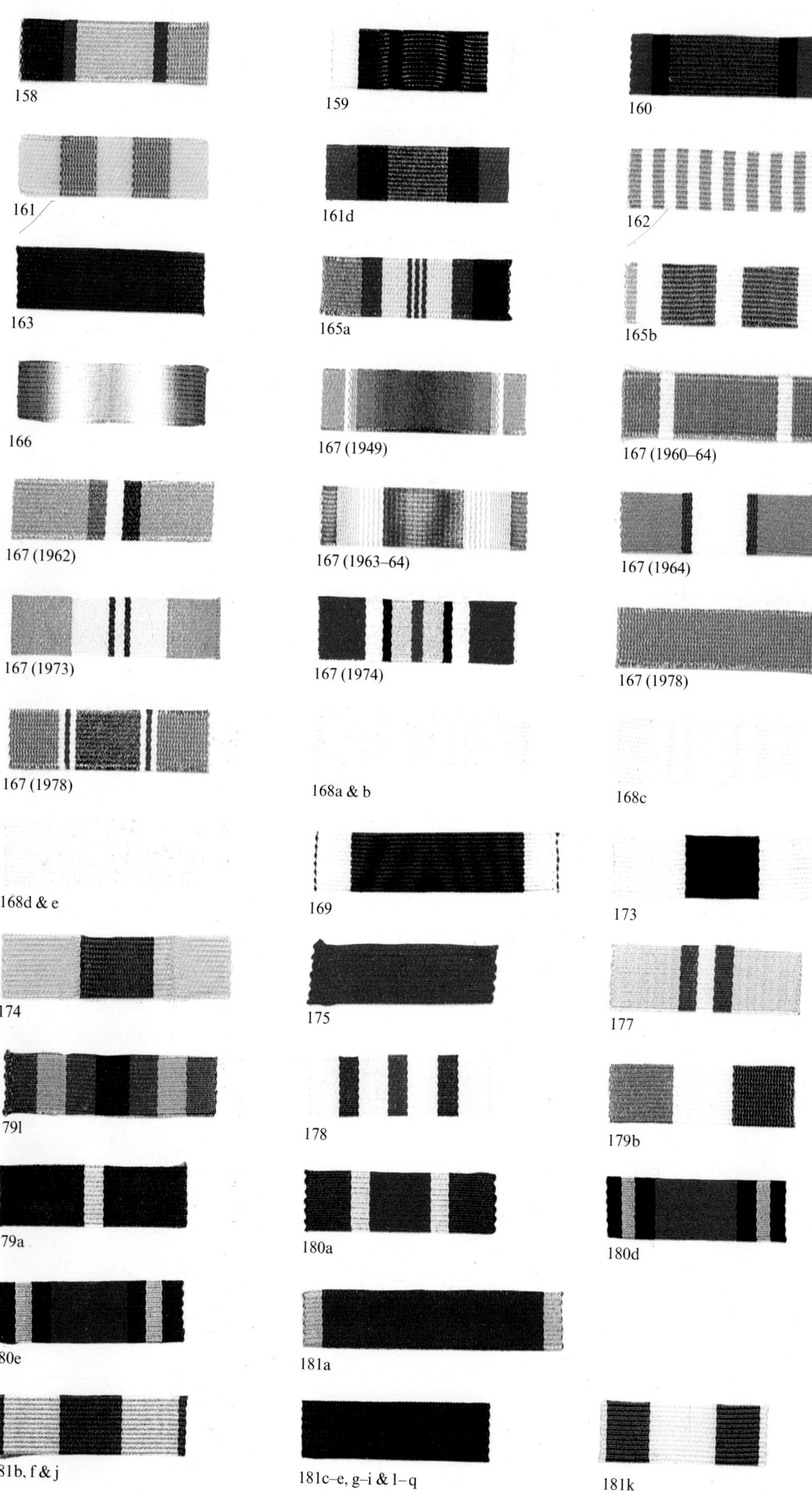

158
159
160
161
161d
162
163
165a
165b
166
167 (1949)
167 (1960–64)
167 (1962)
167 (1963–64)
167 (1964)
167 (1973)
167 (1974)
167 (1978)
167 (1978)
168a & b
168c
168d & e
169
173
174
175
177
179l
178
179b
179a
180a
180d
180e
181a
181b, f & j
181c–e, g–i & l–q
181k

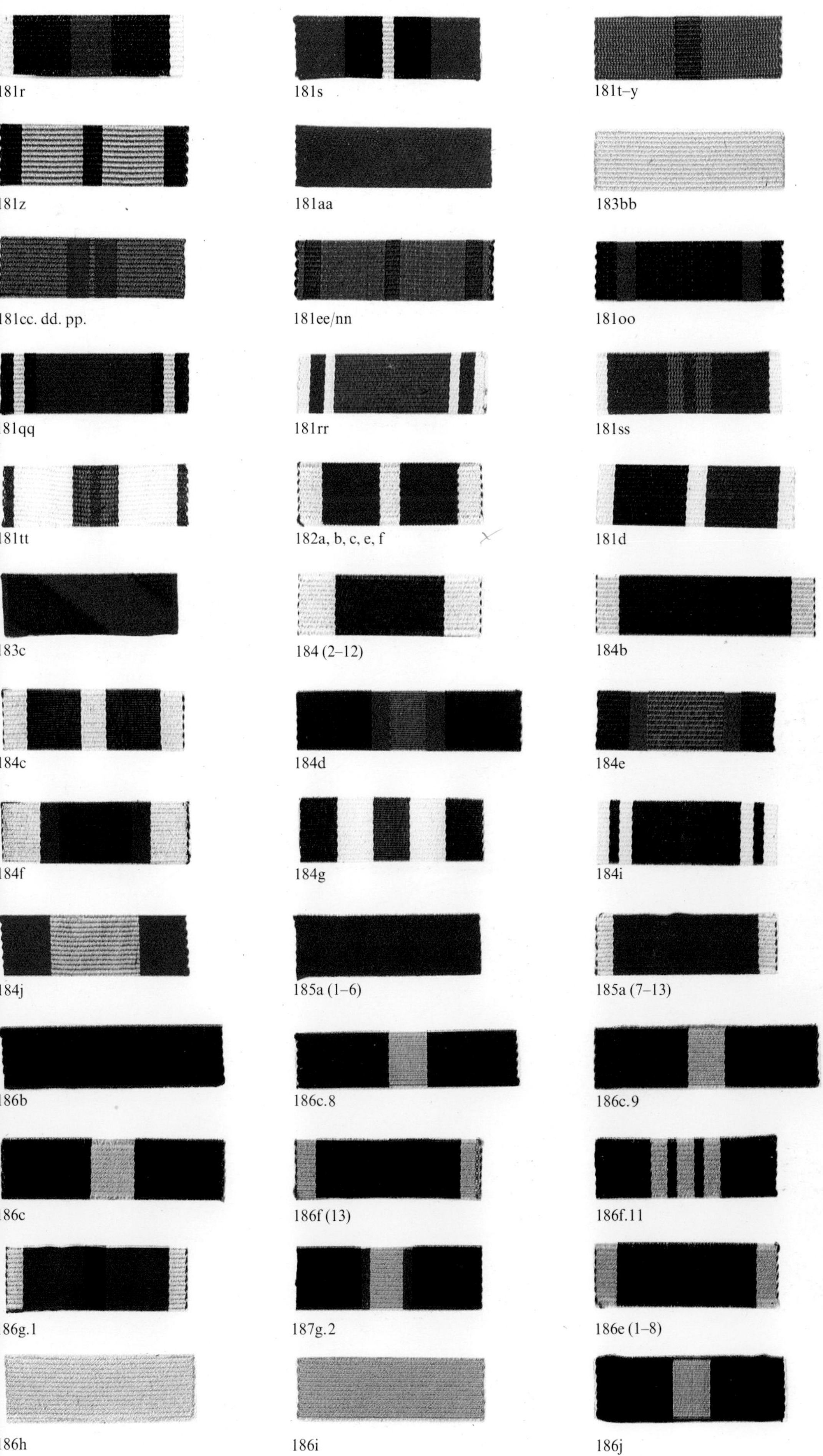
181r
181s
181t–y
181z
181aa
183bb
181cc. dd. pp.
181ee/nn
181oo
181qq
181rr
181ss
181tt
182a, b, c, e, f
181d
183c
184 (2–12)
184b
184c
184d
184e
184f
184g
184i
184j
185a (1–6)
185a (7–13)
186b
186c.8
186c.9
186c
186f (13)
186f.11
186g.1
187g.2
186e (1–8)
186h
186i
186j

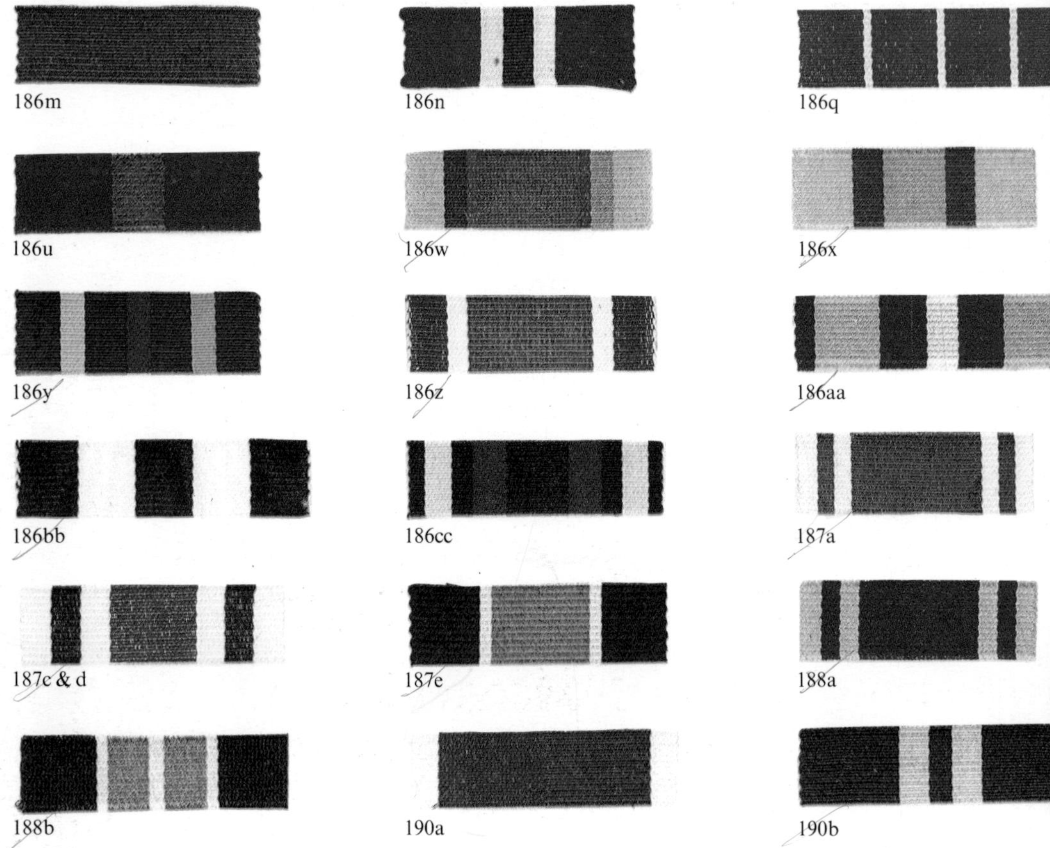
186m
186n
186q
186u
186w
186x
186y
186z
186aa
186bb
186cc
187a
187c & d
187e
188a
188b
190a
190b

# Orders, Decorations and Medals

*with valuations*

# Orders of Knighthood

*Prices of gold insignia are based on the period 1860–87. Earlier insignia can be expected to cost a little more.*

*Complete sets of first- and second-class insignia in their original cases could be expected to cost a little more than the total of any separately quoted stars and badges—this applies to all insignia.*

The dates given are those of the foundation of the orders, and of their becoming obsolete where this applies.

In the case of the lesser orders, insignia are returnable on promotion to a higher class. All collar chains are returnable, though the St Michael and St George could be retained up to 1948.

## 1 The Most Noble Order of the Garter (K.G.) 1348

This is one of the 'great' Orders, the others being the Thistle and the Patrick.

The Garter was founded by King Edward III and as it is the premier order of Great Britain, it commands the very highest respect.

The Order consists of twenty-five Knights only and is the personal gift of the Sovereign and, due to the small number of Knights, it is one of the rarest orders in existence today. Unlike many other orders, the Garter has never been suspended, having been awarded continuously since the middle of the fourteenth century.

In addition to the twenty-five Knights, there are a small number of 'extra' Knights who invariably are non-Christians such as the Emperor of Japan and two past sovereigns of Turkey. Sir Winston Churchill, probably one of the most outstanding commoners to be awarded the Order in recent years, was awarded the insignia originally presented to one of his forebears, namely the 1st Duke of Marlborough, who was admitted to the Order in 1702. The Garter sash is worn over the left shoulder which is opposite to the lesser orders. The motto of the Garter is '*Honi soit qui mal y pense*' or 'Evil be who evil thinks'.

The officially issued insignia of this Order have always been returnable to the Crown by the heirs of the recipients. Before the latter part of the nineteenth century, however, when insignia were more frequently worn than is now the custom, Knights often purchased additional stars and badges at their own expense. This practice can also be explained by the fact that there were no metal stars furnished by the Crown until 1858, and also by the desire of the Knights to have more splendid badges than the rather plain officially issued specimens. Privately commissioned insignia of these orders occasionally appear on the market, the price of these pieces largely depending on their age and quality.

---

*Regarding 1, 2 and 3 (below), the early and more outstanding of the privately made pieces could be expected to cost more. The prices below are for standard insignia similar to those officially awarded.*

*Prices are for insignia without pedigree; insignia* proved *to have been worn by outstanding personalities could be expected to be of more value.*

| | | |
|---|---|---|
| a | Collar chain | £30,000 |
| b | Collar badge (The George) | £17,000 |
| c | Star (in metal, early 20th-century) | £2850 |
| d | Star (embroidered, in VF condition) | £400 |
| e | Sash badge (The Lesser George, early 20th-century) | £7500 |
| f | Garter (with embroidered lettering in VF condition) | £550 |
| g | Garter (with *gold* lettering, buckle and tab) | £1750 |

ORDER OF THE GARTER
*top:* Knight's Collar, collar badge (*The George*),
breast star and sash badge (*Lesser George*)

HONI SOIT QUI MAL Y PENSE

*centre:* The Garter. *below:* The Great George
(superb diamond set eighteenth century piece)

ORDER OF THE GARTER
*left:* A mid-Victorian breast star
*right:* Privately made lesser George badge

## 2 The Most Ancient and the Most Noble Order of the Thistle (K.T.) 1687

The usually accepted date of the institution of this Order is 1687, the Order having been revived by Queen Anne in 1703. However, it has been suggested by some authorities that the Order was founded as far back as 787. This, however, is thought to be a legend and, if it were true, and some believe it is, then it might be said to be senior to the Garter—claims of this nature have been made. The motto of the Order is *'nemo me impune lacessit'* or 'No-one provokes me with impunity'.

The Order is restricted to sixteen distinguished Scotsmen, thus making it more exclusive than the Garter and probably the rarest order in Europe if not the world. Occasionally, extra Knights who are selected members of royal families are awarded the Order. No foreigner has been made a Knight for over two hundred years, with the exception of King Olaf of Norway, who was admitted as an extra Knight in 1962. Unlike the Garter, which is occasionally awarded to non-Christians, the Thistle is restricted in this respect.

As with the Garter, all the insignia are returnable and the only pieces that just occasionally come on to the market are invariably the unofficially produced pieces of years past. Again, as with the Garter, the sash riband is worn over the left shoulder, resting on the right hip.

| | | |
|---|---|---|
| a | Collar chain | £28,000 |
| b | Collar badge | £13,000 |
| c | Star (in metal, early 20th-century) | £2500 |
| d | Star (embroidered, in VF condition) | £400 |
| e | Sash badge (gold) | £3500 |

ORDER OF THE THISTLE
Knight's collar chain with collar badge.
Breast star and sash badge

ORDER OF THE THISTLE
Sash badge

*right:* Breast star (early nineteenth century)

## 3 The Most Illustrious Order of St Patrick (K.P.) 1783–1974

The Order was originally founded as a gesture of goodwill towards Ireland, and made available to Irish peers for distinguished services and to those who could not be admitted to the Order of the Garter.

For the first time since its institution in 1783, the Order of St Patrick now has no Knights as no new non-royal knights have been created since 1922 when the Union of Ireland with Great Britain was dissolved. Three royal Knights, sons of King George V, were created after 1922—the Prince of Wales, later the Duke of Windsor (1927), the Duke of York, later George VI (1936) and the Duke of Gloucester (1934).

During the Second World War, a number of distinguished service leaders whose families were associated with Northern Ireland would probably have qualified as knights. It was suggested that the Order be kept alive by such appointments but the separation of the North and South of Ireland made the revival impracticable. It is ironic that the legend of the Order is *'quis separabit'*—'Who shall separate'! The 9th Earl of Shaftesbury was the longest surviving recipient of the Order; he was awarded the honour in 1911 and died fifty years later in 1961.

Unlike the other two great Orders, the Garter and the Thistle, the sash for this Order is worn as with other lesser orders, over the right shoulder.

| | | |
|---|---|---|
| a | Collar chain | £17,000 |
| b | Collar Badge (as left-hand badge) | £6000 |
| c | Sash badge (as right-hand badge) | £6500 |
| d | Star (in silver/gold) | £1850 |
| e | Star (embroidered, in VF condition) | £300 |

ORDER OF ST. PATRICK
Knight's collar chain, collar badge and sash badge

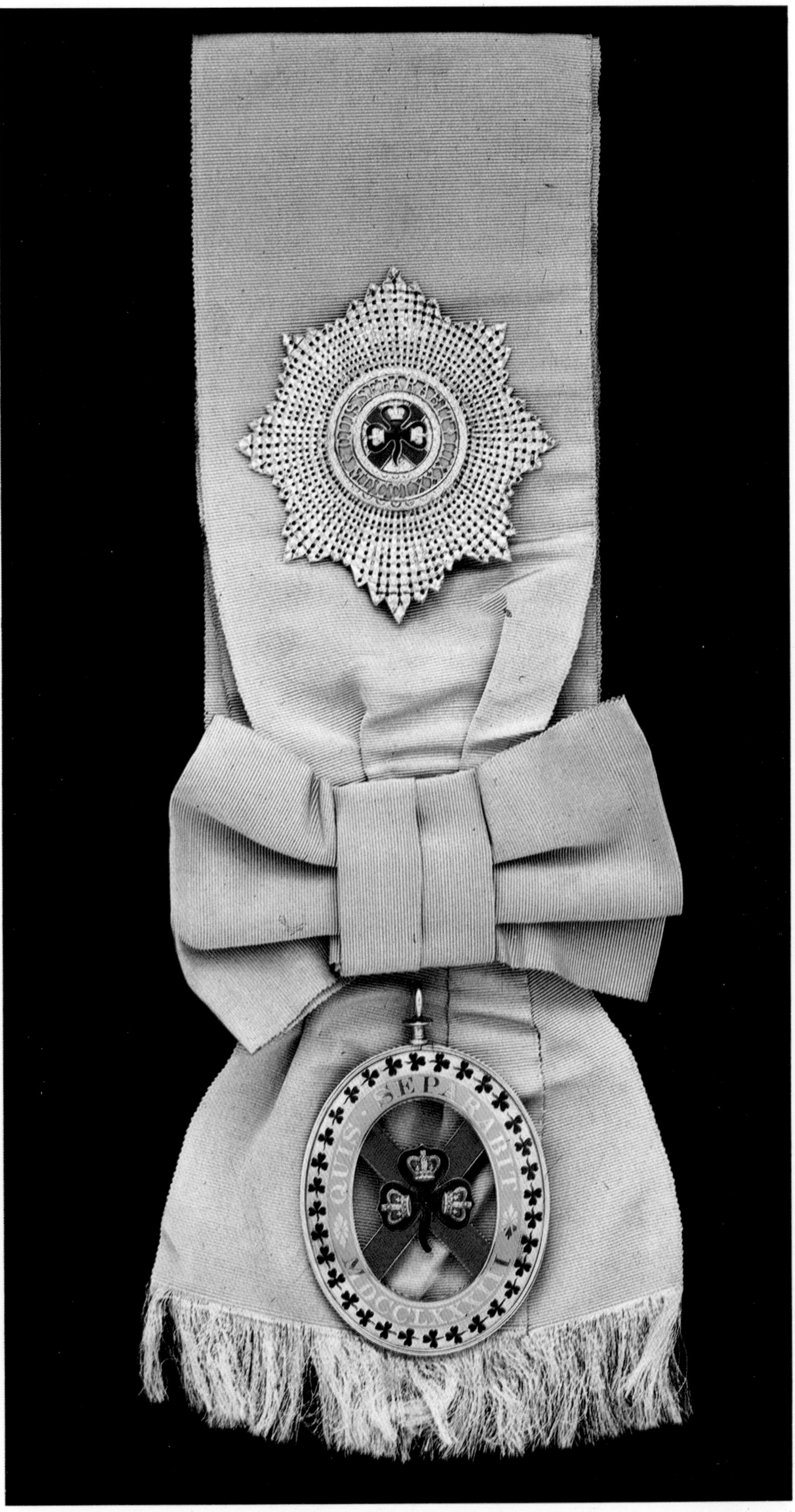


Knight's breast star and sash badge

## 4 The Most Honourable Order of the Bath 1725

The Order was founded during the time of the Prime Minister Sir Robert Walpole as an order with one class and one division only, recipients being known as K.Bs, or simply Knights of the Bath.

The title of the Order always seems remarkably strange to foreigners, but this was derived from the ancient ritual of bathing or cleansing which was symbolic of washing away any impurities before admission to the Order.

In 1815, after the conclusion of the Napoleonic Wars, the Prince Regent (later George IV) found it necessary to reward many distinguished officers of both the Navy and the Army, consequently the Order was enlarged by creating two divisions, military as well as civil, with the military embracing three classes. These were the G.C.B. (Knight Grand Cross), K.C.B. (Knight Commander) and the C.B. (Companion). In 1847 it was found necessary to enlarge the civil division to three classes which then corresponded with the military division. All badges were produced in gold prior to 1887, since when they have always been in silver gilt.

Admission to the Order is currently granted rather sparingly, and since 1971 women have also been admitted. Undoubtedly the Bath is probably the most highly regarded of the lesser orders. The motto of the Order is *'Tria juncta in uno'* 'Three joined in one', namely England, Scotland and Ireland.

Until 1857 the insignia of all grades of both divisions were returnable by the heirs of the recipients and then reissued. However, after that year they were allowed to be retained by the families. These days, the insignia are returnable only upon promotion in the Order although, as with all other orders the collar chain has to be returned.

Knight Grand Cross Collar Chain (Military and Civil)
with a Civil Division badge attached
*centre:* The Knight Grand Cross (Civil) Star and Badge

*opposite:*
ORDER OF THE BATH
Knight Grand Cross Collar Chain, (Military and Civil)
with a Military Division badge attached
*centre:* Knight Grand Cross (Military) Star and Badge

ORDER OF THE BATH

*above:* Knight (left) and Dame Commanders' (right) stars and badges (Military Division)

*below:* Companions' badges (Military) as worn by a gentleman and lady

ORDER OF THE BATH
Dame Commander's badge

Companion's badge (Civil) as worn by a lady

Knight Commander's star (Civil Division)

Dame Commander's star (Civil Division)

Knight Commander's badge (Civil Division)

Companion's badge (Civil) as worn by a gentleman

*Prices for gold badges are based on those issued just prior to 1887, earlier insignia can be expected to be more valuable; complete cased sets would command a further premium of about 10%.*

| | | |
|---|---|---|
| a | Collar chain | £28,000 |
| b | Collar badge | £5000 |
| c | Star (metal) | £3500 |
| d | Star (embroidered, in VF condition) | £300 |
| e | Oval gold sash badge without enamel (similar to the later civil division) | £5000 |

*Insignia after 1815*

MILITARY DIVISION

| | | |
|---|---|---|
| | **Knight Grand Cross (G.C.B.)** | |
| f | Collar chain (gold) | £22,000 |
| g | Collar badge (gold) | £4250 |
| h | Star | £850 |
| i | Star (embroidered, in VF condition) | £225 |
| j | Sash badge (gold and enamel) | £4000 |
| k | Sash badge (silver gilt and enamel) | £1200 |
| | **Knight Commander (K.C.B.)** | |
| l | Star | £450 |
| m | Star (embroidered, in VF condition) | £125 |
| n | Neck badge (gold and enamel) | £1500 |
| o | Neck badge (silver gilt and enamel) | £500 |
| | **Companion (C.B.)** | |
| p | Breast badge (gold and enamel) | £750 |
| q | Breast badge (silver gilt and enamel) | £250 |
| r | Neck badge (silver gilt and enamel) | £225 |

CIVIL DIVISION

| | | |
|---|---|---|
| | **Knight Grand Cross (G.C.B.)** | |
| s | Collar (silver gilt) | £12,000 |
| t | Star (metal) | £500 |
| u | Sash collar badge (gold) | £1850 |
| v | Sash collar badge (silver gilt) | £525 |
| | **Knight Commander (K.C.B.)** | |
| w | Star (metal) | £200 |
| x | Neck badge (gold) | £675 |
| y | Neck badge (silver gilt) | £200 |
| | **Companion (C.B.)** | |
| z | Breast badge (gold) | £425 |
| aa | Breast badge (silver gilt) | £90 |
| bb | Neck badge (silver gilt) | £125 |

## 5 The Royal Guelphic Order 1815–37

Instituted by the Prince Regent (later George IV) and awarded by the Crown of Hanover to both British and Hanoverian servicemen and civilians for distinguished services to Hanover.

By the Hanoverian law of succession, a lady could not ascend the throne, consequently, upon the death of William IV, Queen Victoria could not adopt the title of Sovereign and the Duke of Cumberland, fifth son of George III, became King of Hanover. From then on, the Guelphic Order became a totally Hanoverian award.

As with the Order of the Bath, which the insignia rather resembles from a design point of view, the Order comprised three classes, having both military and civil divisions. The motto of the Order is *'Nec aspera terrent*—'Difficulties do not terrify'.

The majority of the recipients during the early years were distinguished British and Hanoverian officers who had fought Napoleon, many Hanoverian regiments having fought with distinction under Wellington in both the Spanish Peninsula and at Waterloo.

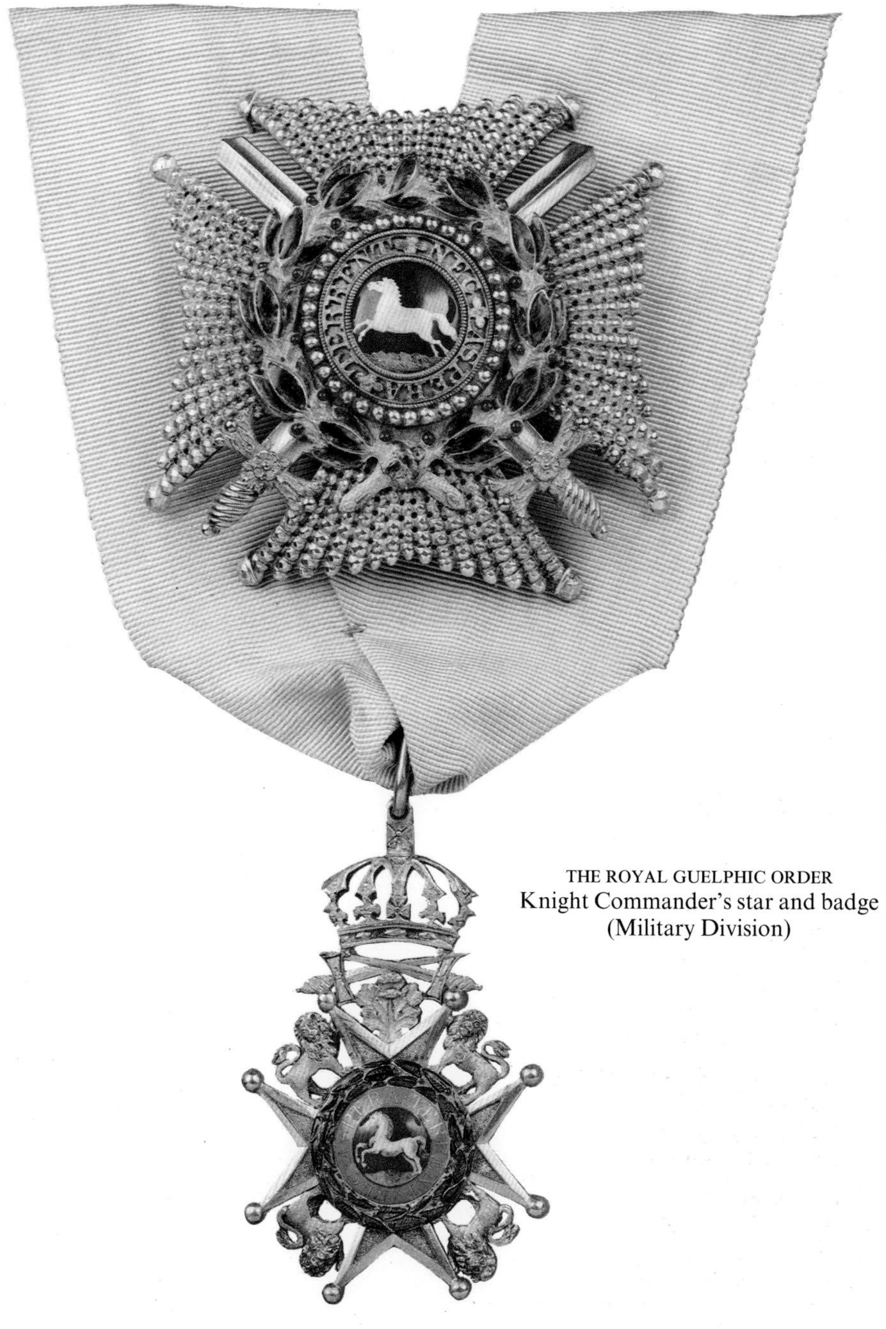

THE ROYAL GUELPHIC ORDER
Knight Commander's star and badge
(Military Division)

The prices of insignia listed below have been based on the period 1815–37, all insignia being London made.

The lower classes of the award, namely the Knights and the Knight Commander, do from time to time come on to the market, particularly the civil ones. However, many military division awards are often accompanied by other decorations.

| | | 1 Military | 2 Civil |
|---|---|---|---|
| | **Knight Grand Cross (G.C.H.)** | | |
| a | Gold collar. *No distinction between military and civil* | £8500 | £8500 |
| b | Silver gilt collar. *No distinction between military and civil* | £4250 | £4250 |
| c | Collar badge (gold and enamel 2.6in dia.) | £4850 | £3850 |
| d | Star | £850 | £700 |
| e | Sash badge (gold and enamel) | £5250 | £4250 |
| | **Knight Commander (K.C.H.)** | | |
| f | Star | £650 | £500 |
| g | Neck badge (gold and enamel) | £1350 | £950 |
| | **Knight** | | |
| h | Breast badge (gold and enamel) | £750 | £600 |
| i | Breast badge (silver and enamel) | £225 | £165 |

## 6 The Most Distinguished Order of St Michael and St George 1818

Founded in 1818 by the Prince Regent, and awarded as a token of appreciation for services rendered by the population of the Ionian Islands in the Mediterranean, which in 1815 had been formed as an independent kingdom under the protection of the United Kingdom. The islands, which were acquired as a result of the Napoleonic Wars, were at that time very strategically placed, thus making them important to Great Britain.

Towards the end of the nineteenth century, due to the growing extent of the British Empire, the Order was then extended to those who had rendered distinguished services in the colonies and in foreign affairs generally. Hence the motto, *'Puspicium melioris aevi*—'Token of a better age'.

As with the Order of the Bath, the St Michael and St George comprises three classes, namely G.C.M.G. (Knight Grand Cross), K.C.M.G. (Knight Commander) and C.M.G. (Companion). The insignia of this Order have never been made returnable except in the cases of promotion. There was one exception, however, the silver gilt collar chain which has only been made returnable upon the death of the recipient since 1948.

As with all British insignia, these were awarded in gold and enamel prior to 1887; at that time Britain went off the 'gold standard', so to speak, since when all awards have been in silver gilt and enamel. In more recent years, the insignia have been awarded to ladies but to date only three Grand Crosses have been issued.

| | | |
|---|---|---|
| | **Knight Grand Cross (G.C.M.G.)** | |
| a | Collar chain (only returnable since 1948) | £1700 |
| b | Star | £600 |
| c | Sash badge (gold and enamel) | £4000 |
| d | Sash badge (silver gilt and enamel) | £750 |
| | **Knight Commander (K.C.M.G.)** | |
| e | Star (introduced 1859) | £350 |
| f | Neck badge (gold and enamel) | £1550 |
| g | Neck badge (silver gilt and enamel) | £300 |
| | **Companion (C.M.G.)** | |
| h | Breast badge (gold and enamel) | £550 |
| i | Breast badge (silver gilt and enamel) | £200 |
| j | Neck badge (silver gilt and enamel) | £200 |

*All prices are based on insignia awarded to gentlemen.*

ORDER OF ST. MICHAEL AND ST. GEORGE
Knight Grand Cross Collar Chain with breast star and sash badge

*opposite:* Knight Commander's star and badge

ORDER OF ST. MICHAEL AND ST. GEORGE
*top:* Dame Commander's badge and star
*below:* Companion's badges (ladies and gentlemen)

*opposite:*
ORDER OF THE STAR OF INDIA
Knight Grand Commander's collar chain and collar badge
with (*centre*) breast star and sash badge

## 7 The Most Exalted Order of the Star of India 1861–1947

Founded in 1861 as a reward for services in connection with India. After the Indian Mutiny of 1857–58, the British Crown accepted responsibility for the administration of the Indian subcontinent, taking over the duties from the private trading company, known as the Honourable East India Company. It was quickly realized that it was necessary to have an order connected solely with India, as a mark of the Government's esteem for the loyal princes and others. The insignia are the most magnificient of all British Orders, especially the Knight Grand Commander (G.C.S.I.), which, as it was awarded to the Viceroy and Indian princes, was of gold and enamel, lavishly set with diamonds.

Prior to the independence of India in 1947, all insignia of this Order were returnable by the hiers of the recipients. However, after 1947, the Order was no longer awarded and the recipients or their families were allowed in certain cases to purchase the star and badges of any of the applicable three classes, but not the Grand Commander gold and enamel collar chain, consequently, these collar chains seldom, if ever, come on to the market.

The first class of this and the Order of the Indian empire was designated Knight Grand Commander, thus removing the Christian designation of Knight Grand Cross, the Order being given mainly to Hindus and Muslims.

| | | |
|---|---|---|
| a | Knight Grand Commander (G.C.S.I.) gold and enamel collar chain | £27,000 |
| b | Knight Grand Commander (G.C.S.I.) star and sash badge | £25,000 |
| c | Knight Commander (K.C.S.I.) star and neck badge | £3750 |
| d | Companion (C.S.I.) breast or neck badge | £1750 |

ORDER OF THE STAR OF INDIA
*left to right:* Knight Commander's badge, star and Companion's neck badge

## 8 The Most Eminent Order of the Indian Empire 1878–1947

Originally this Order consisted of Companions only, but was then enlarged in 1887 to the three traditional classes. This was the second of the Indian orders founded by Queen Victoria when she adopted the title 'Empress of India'. Hence the motto *'Imperatricis auspicus*—Under the auspices of the Empress'.

The Order was discontinued in 1947 due to independence being granted to India and Pakistan; the Order is the fourth and final British Order which has been discontinued owing to political reasons, the others being the Orders of St Patrick, Guelphic and Star of India.

The design of the Order, like the Star of India, came about as it was necessary to omit a cross, which is the traditional basis for the designs of British orders. A cross would not have been accepted by the non-Christian recipients and, consequently, unlike other orders, it did not have a patron saint. The Order was intended to serve as a junior award to the Order of the Star of India, a certain proportion of the Indian Empire Order was awarded to officers of the two services. The third-class badge of this Order, like all other orders, was worn on the breast, the same way as a medal, but in 1917 it was altered for wear around the neck. Prior to the independence of India in 1947, the first and second classes were returnable by the recipients' executors upon their death. However, as with the Star of India, the recipients or their families were allowed to purchase the stars and badges, but not the Knight Grand Commander's silver gilt collar chain.

| | | |
|---|---|---|
| a | Knight Grand Commander (G.C.I.E.) silver gilt collar chain | £6000 |
| b | Knight Grand Commander (G.C.I.E.) star and sash badge | £4250 |
| c | Knight Commander (K.C.I.E.) star and neck badge | £2000 |
| d | Companion (C.I.E.) 1st issue breast badge with 'INDIA' on the petals of the lotus flower | £950 |
| e | Companion (C.I.E.) 2nd issue (smaller size) breast badge | £300 |
| f | Companion (C.I.E.) 3rd issue (smaller size) neck badge | £300 |

ORDER OF THE INDIAN EMPIRE
*top:* Knight Grand Commander's collar chain, breast star and sash badge

*below left to right:* Knight Commander's badge, star
and Companion's (fourth issue) neck badge

## 9 The Royal Family Order

There are three orders (nos. 9, 10 & 11) associated with the Court which are only awarded to ladies. The first is the Royal Family Order, which is worn only by the Queen and the female relatives of the Sovereign: special badges of distinction are awarded to their ladies-in-waiting. The modern Royal Family Order consists of badges set with diamonds which in turn invariably surround the portrait of the Sovereign. These insignia very seldom come on to the market and it would be pointless and even foolhardy to endeavour to price them.

The second was the Order of Victoria and Albert instituted by Queen Victoria in 1862, which was conferred as a special mark of personal regard and favour on both British and foreign members of the Royal Household. There are four classes to the Order, incorporating diamonds and pearls, etc of varying values.

The third order in this series is The Imperial Order of the Crown of India which was introduced in 1878 for award to ladies only for services in connection with the Indian continent. The Order, which was discontinued in 1947 when India and Pakistan became independent, was awarded to female members of the Royal Family, Indian princesses and those connected with the Viceroy of India and the Governors of the various provinces. The Order consisted of one class only, and did not carry any title or precedence, and in spite of its wide coverage, was very seldom awarded. The oval badge is particularly attractive in that it is made of gold and contains diamonds, pearls and turquoises. The Order has always been returnable to the Crown on death, but it seems likely that those in possession of the insignia in 1947 might have been allowed to retain them. Only one or two examples of insignia have appeared on the collectors' market.

---

This Order is worn by the Queen and the female relatives of the Sovereign. Special badges are also given to ladies-in-waiting. These insignia virtually never come on the market.

---

THE ROYAL FAMILY ORDER
George VI issue

## 10 The Royal Order of Victoria & Albert 1862

a 1st class £22,000
b 2nd class £13,000
c 3rd class (4 sections of 5 pearls and 4 diamonds surround the cameo centre, all surmounted by a crown) £9500
d 4th class (interlocking pierced 'V/A' set with small pearls suspended from a crown) £3750

*All insignia are returnable*

THE ROYAL ORDER OF VICTORIA AND ALBERT
1st class

## 11 The Imperial Order of the Crown of India 1878–1947

Breast Badge £8000

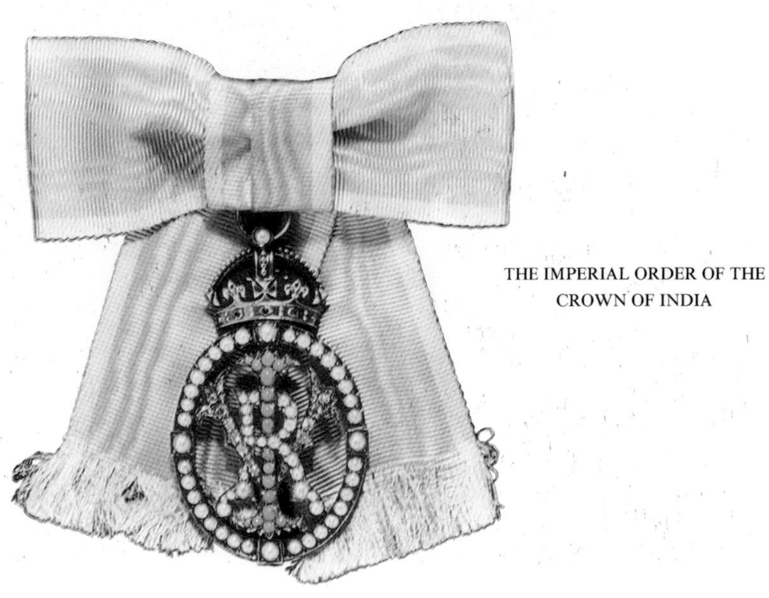

THE IMPERIAL ORDER OF THE CROWN OF INDIA

## 12 The Royal Victorian Order 1896

This was the last of the Orders instituted during the nineteenth century, having been introduced in 1896 towards the very end of the reign of Queen Victoria.

At the time of the introduction of this Order, prime ministers and governments were increasing their influence over the distribution of awards and distinctions. The Victorian Orders and Medals were introduced, therefore, so as to be totally outside the jurisdiction of members of government—the award being the sole prerogative of the Sovereign. From the very beginning, the Order consisted of five classes plus three different classes of medals, which are available to both ladies and gentlemen. In addition, there is the very special and extremely rare distinction known as the Royal Victorian Chain, introduced by Edward VII in 1902, and only awarded, for instance, to selected foreign princes and very high-ranking members of the Royal Household. Needless to say, these Victorian Chains are seldom seen on the market.

All insignia are in silver (gilt) and enamel. The large majority are numbered and are returnable on promotion.

| | | 1 Gentleman | 2 Ladies |
|---|---|---|---|
| a | Knight Grand Cross (G.C.V.O.) collar chain | £7500 | £9000 |
| b | Knight Grand Cross (G.C.V.O.) sash badge and breast star | £650 | £1200 |
| c | Knight Commander (K.C.V.O.) neck badge and breast star | £475 | £625 |
| d | Commander (C.V.O.) neck badge | £200 | £250 |
| e | Member (4th class) (M.V.O.) breast badge | £90 | £115 |
| f | Member (5th class) (M.V.O.) breast badge | £80 | £100 |

*Ladies' insignia are similar in size to the gentlemen's but the collar is smaller, the G.C.V.O. star is also slightly smaller, the sash only is 2.25in wide. The badges of the lower grades are suspended from a bow except when worn in uniform.*

THE ROYAL VICTORIAN ORDER
Knight Grand Cross Collar Chain with sash badge and breast star

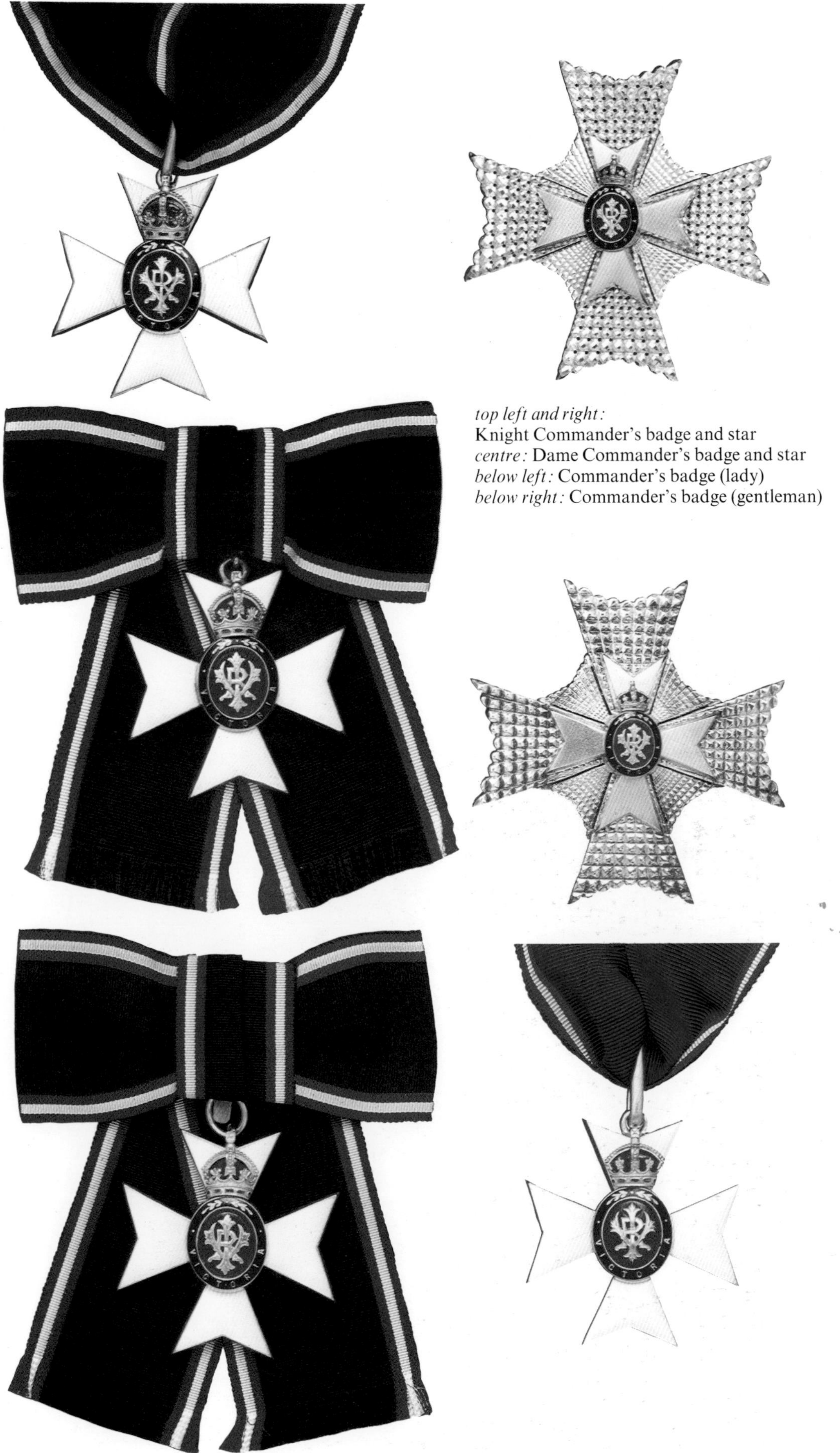


*top left and right:*
Knight Commander's badge and star
*centre:* Dame Commander's badge and star
*below left:* Commander's badge (lady)
*below right:* Commander's badge (gentleman)

THE ROYAL VICTORIAN ORDER
*top left:* Member's badge, 4th class (lady)
*top right:* Member's badge, 4th class
*below left:* Member's badge, 5th class
*below right:* Member's badge, 5th class (lady)

## 13 The Royal Victorian Medal

| | | |
|---|---|---|
| | *Victoria* | |
| a | Silver | £65 |
| b | Bronze | £50 |
| | *Edward VII* | |
| c | Silver | £65 |
| d | Bronze | £45 |
| | *George V* | |
| e | Silver gilt | £60 |
| f | Silver | £50 |
| g | Bronze | £30 |
| | *Edward VIII* | |
| h | Silver (2 issued) | £1000 |
| | *George VI* | |
| i | Silver gilt | £60 |
| j | Silver | £45 |
| k | Bronze (4 issued) | £575 |
| | *Elizabeth II* | |
| l | Silver gilt | £75 |
| m | Silver | £60 |
| n | Bronze | £45 |

MEDALS OF THE ROYAL VICTORIAN ORDER (*Elizabeth II issue*)
*left:* In silver gilt
*right:* In silver
(Upper pair as worn by a lady; lower
two ribbons as awarded to foreigners)

## 14 The Royal Victorian Chain 1902

| | | |
|---|---|---|
| a | Gentlemen's collar with standard C.V.O. badge | £6500 |
| b | Gentlemen's collar (1921 issue with diamonds to crown and cypher) | £12,000 |
| c | Ladies' bow arrangement (1902–21 with a standard C.V.O. badge without diamonds) | £6500 |
| d | Ladies' bow arrangement (1921 issue with diamonds to crown and cypher) | £12,000 |

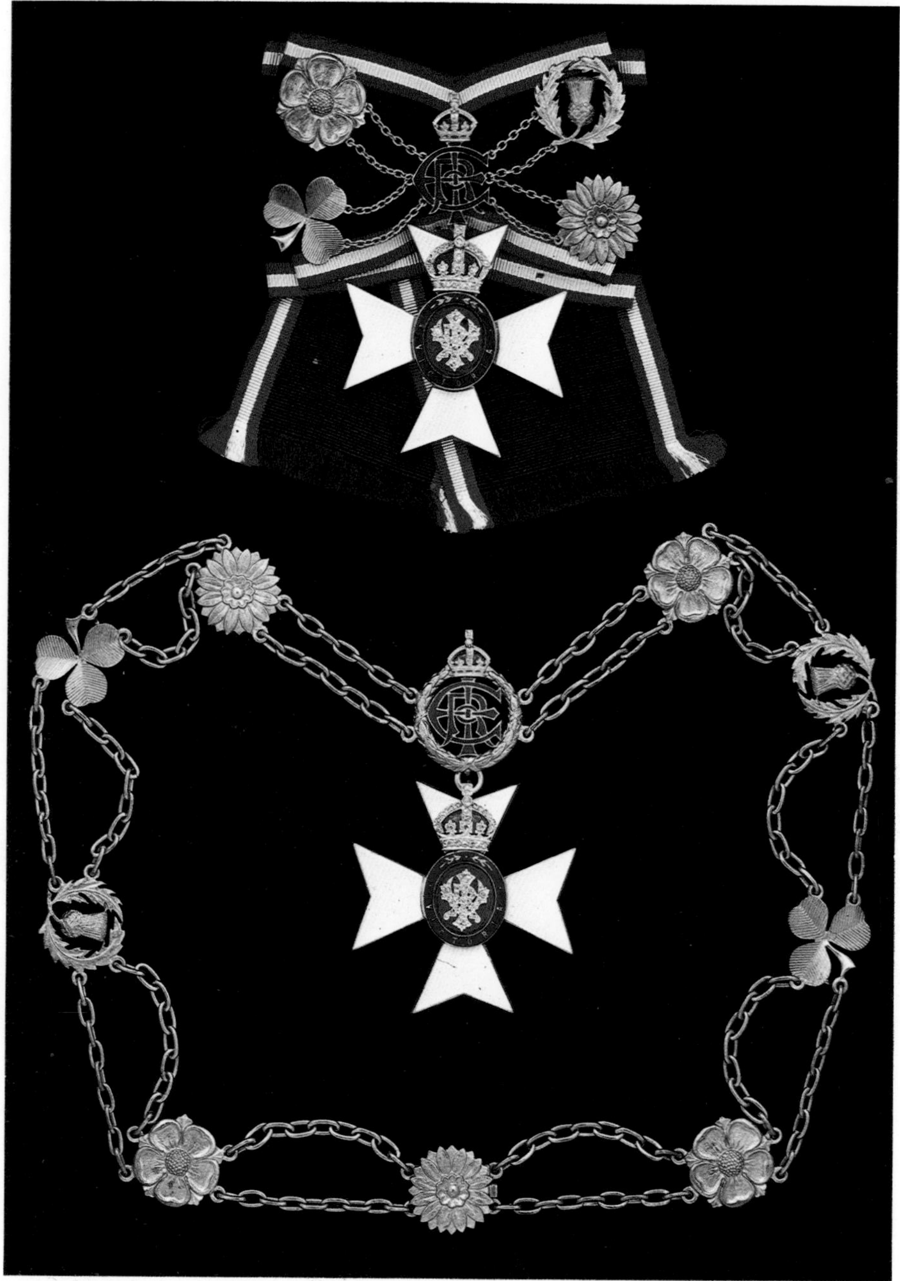

ROYAL VICTORIAN CHAIN
*top:* As worn by a lady
*below:* As worn by a gentleman

## 15 The Order of Merit 1902

In spite of the fact that this is a relatively modern order, it is one of the most coveted of British distinctions. It was introduced by King Edward VII in 1902 being a very special distinction awarded to those supreme in the fields of art, music and literature, and is also, from time to time, awarded to military leaders in time of war. The military division is distinguished by crossed swords that pass through the centre of the neck badge. This is another order which again is limited, this time to twenty-four members as well as an additional limited number of foreign recipients. As with the Royal Victorian Order, the Order of Merit is the sole gift of the Sovereign but carries no rank apart from the initials O.M. after the name. This award is also presented to ladies, recipients being Florence Nightingale in 1905, Professor Dorothy Hodgkin in 1965 and Dame Veronica Wedgwood in 1969. Other well-known public figures that were given this distinction were Sir Winston Churchill, General Eisenhower (later President of the USA), Field Marshal Alexander and Admiral of the Fleet Earl Mountbatten. The riband is interesting in that the blue represents the Order of the Garter, and the red, the Order of the Bath.

It is particularly difficult to assess the value of the military division of this Order, as invariably when they do appear on the market they are accompanied by other decorations and medals forming part of a group.

The numbers awarded during the different reigns are shown in brackets, but in addition, nine honorary awards have been presented, as follows:
Edward VII (3), George V (2), George VI (2) and E. II R. (2).

| | *Military* | | | *Civil* | |
|---|---|---|---|---|---|
| a | Edward VII (7) | £4250 | e | Edward VII (17) | £3000 |
| b | George V (7) | £4250 | f | George V (28) | £2500 |
| c | George VI (8) | £4250 | g | George VI (22) | £2750 |
| d | Elizabeth II (2) | £5750 | h | Elizabeth II (41) | £2000 |

THE ORDER OF MERIT
*left:* (Elizabeth II *reverse,* Civil Division)

*right:*
Civil Division, as worn by a lady (*obverse*)

## 16 The Most Excellent Order of the British Empire 1917

This is the junior of all the British Orders, having been founded as recently as 1917. The Order was introduced owing to the very large demand for honours and awards created by the First World War—the Order of the Bath (military division) having been created in 1815 for the very same reasons following the Napoleonic Wars. The Order, as well as the Medals of the Order, is awarded for service to the State and Commonwealth generally, and is given to a very wide range of people (both civilians and service personnel) in all walks of life for valuable work in the social services and local government.

---

When the Order was instituted in 1917, Britannia appeared in the centres of both stars and badges. The riband was purple, with a central scarlet stripe added for the military division. After 1936, joint effigies of King George V and Queen Mary replaced Britannia, the rays of the stars were altered from a fluted effect to faceted or chipped and the riband was changed to rose pink with pearl-grey edges. While the insignia for both the civil and military divisions is the same, the riband for the latter includes an additional central pearl-grey stripe.

Ladies' insignia are similar to the gentlemen's but the collar and G.B.E. star are smaller, the sash is 2.25in in width, and the badges of the lower grades are suspended from a bow, except when worn in uniform.

Generally speaking, the insignia are readily available on the collectors' market, although the Grand Crosses are a little scarce in spite of the comparatively large numbers that were awarded, particularly in the earlier years.

| | | 1 *1st type* | 2 *2nd type* |
|---|---|---|---|
| | *Gentlemen* | | |
| a | Knight Grand Cross (G.B.E.) collar. *Returnable* | £6000 | £6000 |
| b | Knight Grand Cross (G.B.E.) sash badge and star | £950 | £1000 |
| c | Knight Commander (K.B.E.) neck badge and star | £325 | £350 |
| d | Commander (C.B.E.) neck badge | £95 | £105 |
| e | Officer (O.B.E.) breast badge | £35 | £40 |
| f | Member (M.B.E.) breast badge | £35 | £40 |
| | *Ladies* | | |
| g | Dame Grand Cross (G.B.E.) collar. *Returnable* | £7500 | £7500 |
| h | Dame Grand Cross (G.B.E.) sash badge and star | £1100 | £1150 |
| i | Dame Commander (D.B.E.) neck/breast badge and star | £450 | £500 |
| j | Commander (C.B.E.) neck/breast badge | £125 | £135 |
| k | Officer (O.B.E.) breast badge | £45 | £50 |
| l | Member (M.B.E.) breast badge | £45 | £50 |

ORDER OF THE BRITISH EMPIRE
Commander's badge, *left:* lady *right:* gentleman

ORDER OF THE BRITISH EMPIRE

Knight and Dame Commander's badges and stars (*Civil and Military Divisions, 2nd type*)

*below:* Knight Grand Cross Collar Chain with breast star and sash badge

## 17 Medal of the Order of the British Empire 1917 Medal of the Order of the British Empire for Gallantry 1922 Medal of the Order of the British Empire for Meritorious Service 1922

The medal of the Order of the British Empire was introduced in 1917 at the same time as the Order of the British Empire was established. Originally issued in one division only, but in 1918 a military division was created for which the medals were the same but the ribands had a central red stripe. The original issue was unusually small, the medal being just over 1in in diameter. A total of almost 2000 were awarded between 1917 and 1922, when it was replaced by the larger British Empire Medals for Gallantry and Meritorious service.

The medal of the Order of the British Empire for Gallantry, normally referred to as the Empire Gallantry Medal, was originally introduced in 1922. Prior to 1940, when the Gallantry Medal was superseded by the George Cross, the medal had been

awarded on 130 occasions only. The decoration has two divisions, military and civil, in the same way as the insignia of the Order of the British Empire. This medal replaced the original British Empire Medal which had been introduced in 1917.

The Medal for Meritorious Service is an identical medal to that issued in 1922 for gallantry except that the obverse exergue reads 'Meritorious Service' as opposed to 'Gallantry'. Unlike the gallantry medal, which was superseded by the George Cross, the award for meritorious service is still given. Apart from the wording, there was one other small difference—the gallantry medal had a laurel leaf suspender, while the meritorious service medal had an oak leaf suspender. In 1957, an emblem was introduced for wear on the riband to denote gallantry, which was superseded in 1974 by the Queen's Gallantry Medal.

**17 Medals of the Order of the British Empire 1917 1922**

| | | |
|---|---|---|
| a | *1st type* 1917–1922 | £60 |
| | *2nd type* 1922 | |
| b | George V for Gallantry | £475 |
| c | George V for Meritorious Service | £125 |
| d | George VI for Gallantry (superseded by the G.C. in 1940) | £550 |
| e | George VI for Meritorious Service | £65 |
| f | E.IIR. for Meritorious Service | £50 |
| g | E.IIR. with Gallantry emblem (civilians) | £200 |
| h | E.IIR with Gallantry emblem (armed forces) | £300 |

ORDER OF THE BRITISH EMPIRE
The Knight Commander's badge and star, 1st type
(Civil Division)

*opposite:*
*top:* ORDER OF THE BRITISH EMPIRE
Officers' and Members' badges (Civil and Military Divisions)
as worn by gentlemen and ladies

*below:* BRITISH EMPIRE MEDALS
Military and Civil Divisions as worn by gentlemen
and ladies; the left depicting the Gallantry Emblem

## 18 The Order of the Companion of Honour

This is sometimes regarded as a junior Order of Merit which had been introduced in 1902. The C.H. badge was founded by King George V in 1917 at the same time as the Order of the British Empire. It was restricted to fifty companions but increased to sixty-five members in 1943, and is awarded to men or women who perform special services of national importance.

The award is made on the recommendation of prime ministers of the countries of the British Commonwealth, in accordance with the following statutory quotas:

UK—45
Australia—7
New Zealand—2
Other Commonwealth countries—11.

In over half a century, very few recipients have received both the Order of Merit and the Companion of Honour, but among those who have are Lord Atlee, Field Marshal Smutts, Walter de la Mare, Henry Moore, Benjamin Britten, Sir Winston Churchill, G. P. Gooch, Lord Blackett and E. M. Forster.

£900

COMPANION OF HONOUR
*left:* As worn by a lady
*right:* As worn by a gentleman (showing reverse of the badge)

## 19 The Baronet's Badge

The first badge of this Order was instituted in 1629 by the Baronets of Scotland who were known as 'Baronets of Nova Scotia', owing to a grant of lands in Nova Scotia made to them by James I in 1624. It was almost three hundred years before King George V granted permission for the Baronets of England, Ireland, Great Britain and of the United Kingdom to wear distinctive badges to indicate their rank.

The Scottish Baronets wore a badge with a distinctive design, which was a crowned shield carrying the cross of St Andrew. The remaining badges authorized in 1929 contain on a central shield the crowned arms of Ulster, surrounded by a border of roses (England), of shamrocks (Ireland), of roses and thistles combined (Great Britain), or roses, thistles and shamrocks combined (United Kingdom).

| | *Baronets of:* | | | |
|---|---|---|---|---|
| a | Scotland (Nova Scotia) late 18th and early 19th century examples in gold | | | £2000 |
| b | Scotland (Nova Scotia) late 19th and 20th century example in silver gilt | | | £650 |
| c | England (rose surround) | ,, | ,, | £750 |
| d | Ireland (shamrock surround) | ,, | ,, | £750 |
| e | Great Britain (rose and thistle surround) | ,, | ,, | £650 |
| f | United Kingdom (rose, thistle and shamrock surround) | ,, | ,, | £375 |

THE BARONET'S BADGE OF NOVA SCOTIA
*(late eighteenth century)*

## 20 The Knight Bachelor's Badge 1929

Authorized by King George V in 1929 at the same time as the later issue of Baronet's badges. The Imperial Society of Knights Bachelors obtained the permission of the King to wear a distinctive badge so as to distinguish their rank, thus bringing them into line with the Baronets. The first model was of a larger type worn on the breast by means of a reverse pin, this measuring 3in × 2in. It was then reduced in size and much more recently it has been reduced even further and adapted for wear around the neck from a riband. The title 'Knight Bachelor' was introduced by King Henry III to signify that the title dies with the holder.

| | | |
|---|---|---|
| a | 1st type (1926) | £80 |
| b | 2nd type (smaller) | £85 |
| c | 3rd type (smaller) neck badge (1974) | £100 |

KNIGHT BACHELOR'S BADGE
3rd type neck badge

## 21 The Order of St John of Jerusalem 1888

This Order was incorporated by Royal Charter during the reign of Victoria in 1888. The insignia is unique in that it is awarded by the Order itself and not by the Sovereign or the Crown, although the Queen is Sovereign Head or patron of the Order. As a result, the Order can be regarded as a semi-private order.

The Order is given for voluntary work in connection with the priory's activities in hospitals, and ambulance and relief work. Recipients who are not British subjects, or who are non-Christians, are made associates of the Order, and their insignia are distinguished by the fact that the normal plain black watered riband has a central white stripe.

| | | 1 *Silver* | 2 *Base metal* |
|---|---|---|---|
| a | Bailiff Grand Cross, sash badge and star | £500 | £400 |
| b | Dame Grand Cross, sash badge and star | £550 | £450 |
| c | Knight of Justice, neck badge and star | £225 | £175 |
| d | Dame of Justice, breast badge and star | £250 | £200 |
| e | Knight of Grace, neck badge and star | £200 | £150 |
| f | Dame of Grace, breast badge and star | £225 | £175 |
| g | Commander (Brother), neck badge | £85 | £60 |
| h | Commander (Sister), breast badge | £85 | £60 |
| i | Officer (Brother), breast badge | £45 | £30 |
| j | Officer (Sister), breast badge | £45 | £30 |
| k | Serving Brother, breast badge | £65 | £40 |
| l | Serving Sister, breast badge | £65 | £40 |

## 22 The Order of the Dooranie Empire (Afghanistan) 1839

This Order has been included here as, when it was originally instituted in 1839 by the Shah of Afghanistan, it was to be conferred as a reward to British officers only for services to Afghanistan. British officers were awarded 5 first class, 19 second and 36 third class, the insignia being an imitation of the Guelphic Order of Hanover. Insignia of the Order, more particularly the third class, do from time to time come on to the market, and are often associated with groups. (The campaign medal awarded at that time is No. 86.)

| | | |
|---|---|---|
| a | Grand Cross, star and badge | £7500 |
| b | Knight Commander, star and badge | £3750 |
| c | Commander | £1250 |

*Prices are based on 1839 issues proved to British officers.*

# Decorations

*Prices for gallantry awards are based on general citations (where applicable), ie, without detail in the* London Gazette *of a specific act of gallantry. Prices can be considerably enhanced by the particular act of gallantry, the rarity of the award for a particular campaign, combinations of decorations in a group being another important factor. Readers* must *bear in mind that the undermentioned prices are* base *prices.*

*Readers are recommended to study* British Gallantry Awards *by P. E. Abbott and J. M. A. Tamplin for a very comprehensive account of gallantry awards.*

## 23 The Victoria Cross 1856

23

This, the foremost British and Commonwealth gallantry decoration, is awarded for very exceptional gallantry and, as such, is the most prized gallantry award that any subject of the realm can earn.

Introduced in 1856 towards the end of the Crimean War, and made retrospective to 1854, it was deemed by Queen Victoria that the cross should be simple in design and must be made out of the bronze cannon captured from the Russians during the Crimean War. Queen Victoria took a great deal of interest in the award and personally invested 111 Crimea recipients at a parade held in Hyde Park in June 1857. There are many interesting facets to the V.C. for instance, at one time recipients from the Navy wore their award suspended from a navy blue riband and the Army from a crimson riband, the latter being identical to the Army Long Service Medal. In 1916 a miniature of the cross was added to the riband in undress uniform so as to make the award more distinctive, and in 1918 the crimson riband was adopted by all services.

A total of 1354 awards have been given, which includes three bars and from the time of institution until 1908, eight had been forfeited for misconduct. The Army have been awarded 832, the Royal Navy 107, the RAF 31, the remainder being awarded to Commonwealth units. The youngest recipient was only just over fifteen years of age and the oldest sixty-nine. Three have been awarded to fathers and sons, while four have been awarded to brothers.

This is probably the most difficult item of all to value, as so much depends on various factors, such as the branch to which awarded (Navy, Army, RAF, Imperial, Commonwealth or Indian troops); the regiment in which the recipient was serving and the total number awarded to the regiment; the theatre of war and the number awarded for the particular action; the citation details; whether officer or other rank; the condition; the composition and number of other medals that might accompany the award and the biographical details of the recipient. Under these circumstances, one can only suggest after having consulted records over the last twenty-five years, a minimum price of £8000 which would represent a V.C. for the mutiny awarded to, for instance, the Madras Fusiliers, but this would be an award which might have been balloted for, therefore not as desirable as a direct award. By comparison, an award to a Regiment of Foot for, say, the First World War on the Western Front with an average citation could be in the region of £10,500.

24

## 24 The New Zealand Cross 1869

This decoration for gallantry is unique to the Commonwealth of New Zealand and was awarded on twenty-three occasions only for bravery during the period of the second Maori war which lasted from 1860–72, although, in actual fact, the last award was not approved until as late as 1910.

The decoration came about through an Order in Council made at Government House, Wellington on the 10th March 1869, it being the intention of New Zealand that this would be a purely local and unofficial award, in the same manner as those awarded by societies such as the Royal Geographical and Royal Humane, and therefore not to be confused or compared with those awards issued by the Crown. The award came about as local volunteer forces did not qualify for the Victoria Cross.

Awards were made immediately and before the approval of London could be obtained, whereupon the Secratary of State in London, Earl Granville, reacted rather promptly and sent a despatch to the Governor which read, 'I am unwillingly constrained to observe that in complying with this natural desire to reward local forces, you have overstepped the limits of the authority confided to you by Her Majesty. The authority inherent in the Queen as the fountain head of honour throughout her empire has never been delegated to you and you are, therefore, not competent as Her Majesty's representative to create any of those titular or decorative distinctions which, in the British Empire, have their source, and are valuable because they have their source, in the grace of the Sovereign.' After this rather severe dressing down, the Queen eventually gave her blessing to the New Zealand Cross, but, due to the fact that the New Zealand local forces were disbanded later on, the Cross by 1911 had fallen into disuse. The riband was the same as the V.C. but without the later bronze emblem.

£20,000

25

## 25 The George Cross 1940

Instituted in September 1940 at the height of the bombing of UK cities by the German Air Force, the G.C. was intended as a reward for civilians in all walks of life and for members of the armed forces for acts of gallantry arising from enemy action (but note, not for services in the face of the enemy). The award was, from the very outset, a prestigious award ranking immediately after the Victoria Cross.

One hundred and fifty one have been awarded since 1940, which excludes those awarded in exchange for the Empire Gallantry Medal, the Albert Medal and the Edward Medal as well as the unique award to the island of Malta. In all, four have been awarded to women.

The exchange awards (112) are not so sought after or valuable, the price structure being:

| | | |
|---|---|---|
| a | Service awards prior to 1940 (ie exchange awards) | £3000 |
| b | Civilian awards prior to 1940 (ie exchange awards) | £2500 |
| c | Service awards from 1940 | £6750 |
| d | Civilian awards from 1940 | £5750 |

## 26 The Distinguished Service Order 1886

26

Following the campaigns of the mid-nineteenth century, such as the Crimea and the Indian Mutiny, it was realized that there was no adequate reward for distinguished services for presentation to junior officers, apart from the Victoria Cross—in the case of senior officers, membership to the Order of the Bath, was available. As a result, the D.S.O. was introduced. The design has always remained constant with the exception of the reverse centre, the cypher of the sovereign varying as needs be. Originally, the award was manufactured in gold and enamel, but two to three years later, in 1889, it was changed to silver gilt and enamel, in common with the other British awards. Naturally, awards in gold are extremely rare, as indeed are those awarded during the reign of Edward VII, due to the fact that no major wars took part in his reign.

A bar is attached to the centre of the riband and a rosette to the riband when worn in undress uniform to denote second awards; the maximum number of bars to one cross is three, thus representing four D.S.Os, only sixteen have ever been awarded, seven for the First World War, eight for the Second World War and one for Korea.

| | | | *In a group with named medals** | |
|---|---|---|---|---|
| | | 1 *Unnamed Single* | 2 *General Citation* | 3 *Average Citation* |
| a | Victoria (gold—153) | £1100 | £1250 | £1500 |
| b | Victoria (silver gilt) | £375 | £450 | £500 |
| c | Edward VII | £950 | £1100 | £1500 |
| d | George V | £200 | £250 | £300 |
| e | George VI | £300 | £375 | £450 |
| f | George VI (2nd type G.R.VI cypher) | £750 | £900 | £1200 |
| g | E.IIR. | £650 | £800 | £1100 |

*(* Value of other medals in groups should be added)*

## 27 The Imperial Service Order and Medals 1902

Prior to the creation of the Order of the British Empire in 1917, there was no way of rewarding the efforts of the very many lesser members of the civil service in both administrative and clerical posts throughout the country, and indeed the empire. The Imperial Service Order was established by King Edward VII in 1902 so as to fill this gap in the rewards system. In August 1908, the Order was extended so as to include women and, as a result, its scope was considerably widened.

Twenty-five years' service is the normal requirement before an individual can be admitted to the Order, although this was reduced to twenty years in certain outposts, such as India. A medal to the Order was also created; the first medals of the Order were of the same design as the badges, but were executed in silver and bronze

27 a 27 m–o

instead of silver and gold. During the reign of George V, however, the medal of the Order was altered to the traditional circular device.

| | *Order* | |
|---|---|---|
| a | Edward VII (Gentlemen) | £90 |
| b | Edward VII (Ladies) | £275 |
| c | George V (Gentlemen) | £70 |
| d | George V (Ladies) | £200 |
| e | George VI (Gentlemen) | £75 |
| f | George VI (Ladies) | £150 |
| g | E.IIR. (Gentlemen) | £70 |
| h | E.IIR. (Ladies) | £100 |

| | *Medal* | |
|---|---|---|
| i | Edward VII (Gentlemen) | £30 |
| j | Edward VII (Ladies) | £95 |
| k | George V (Gentlemen) (1st issue, star shaped) | £20 |
| l | George V (Ladies, star-shaped) | £90 |
| m | George V (2nd issue, circular medal) | £15 |
| n | George VI | £15 |
| o | E.IIR, | £15 |

## 28 The Indian Order of Merit 1837

This is the oldest gallantry award, having been introduced as far back as 1837 by the Honourable East India Company, who at that time was responsible for the administration of the Indian subcontinent. However, it did not become an official award until after the H.E.I. Company's forces were taken over by the Crown following the conclusion of the Indian Mutiny.

Three classes were originally introduced, the first in gold, and the second and third basically in silver, all with obverse centres enamelled. Recipients were entitled to higher pensions upon retirement. In 1902, a civil division of the Order was introduced to correspond with the military division. In 1911, Indian troops became eligible for the Victoria Cross and the first class in gold was abolished, so the remaining two classes were promoted to first and second class. The civil division which had been introduced in 1902 was reduced to one class only in 1939, as was the military division in 1944. The award was originally known as the 'Order of Merit'

28

but, upon the introduction of the British Order of Merit in 1902 by King Edward VII, the title of this Order was altered to read the 'Indian Order of Merit'.

---

*Military*

Centres read: 'Reward of Valour' unless stated otherwise.

| Period | Class | Description | | Price |
|---|---|---|---|---|
| 1837–1912: | 1st Class | in gold, *42 awarded.* | a | £900 |
| | 2nd Class | in silver with a gold centre and wreath, *130 awarded.* | b | £400 |
| | 3rd Class | in silver, *2740 awarded.* | c | £75 |
| 1912–1939: | 1st Class | in silver with a gold centre and wreath, reverse engraved '1st Class', *26 awarded.* | d | £850 |
| | 2nd Class | in silver, reverse engraved '2nd Class', *1215 awarded.* | e | £95 |
| 1939–1945: | 1st Class | in silver with a gold centre and wreath, reading 'Reward of Gallantry', Reverse engraved '1st Class', *2 awarded.* | f | £2500 |
| 1939–1944: | 2nd Class | in silver, centre reading 'Reward for Gallantry', Reverse engraved '2nd Class', *332 awarded.* | g | £250 |
| 1945–1947: | | Single Class only, in silver with a gold centre and wreath *and a crown above the laurel wreath*, centre reading 'Reward for Gallantry', diameter of the whole increased to 1 7/10in. | h | £350 |

*Civil*

Centres of all read 'For Bravery'. However the 1902–1939 issues are 1 3/16in in diameter.

| Period | Description | | Price |
|---|---|---|---|
| 1902–1939: | 1st Class in gold with ERI or GRI cyphers, *none awarded.* | i | — |
| | 2nd Class in silver with a gold centre, *none awarded.* | j | — |
| | 3rd Class in silver, *29 awarded.* | k | £550 |
| 1939–1947: | Single Class, reduced to 1in diameter in silver with a gold centre and wreath, *10 awarded.* | l | £900 |

ALL PRICES BASED ON THE ASSUMPTION THAT THE AWARD IS COMPLETE WITH THE ISSUED RIBAND BUCKLE. NUMBERS ISSUED ARE APPROXIMATE—SEE 2nd EDITION OF 'BRITISH GALLANTRY AWARDS' FOR MORE PRECISE INFORMATION.

---

## 29 The Royal Red Cross

Prior to the Egyptian Campaign of 1882–89, nurses had not been considered eligible for war medals; however, it was decided that they would qualify for campaign medals, which then raised the question of a special distinction. As a result, Queen Victoria in 1883 approved the institution of the Royal Red Cross for award to British and foreign ladies for exceptional service in the field of naval and military nursing. When first issued, the award was in gold and enamel but, after 1887, in common with other British decorations, the awards were issued in silver gilt and enamel. Some 240 were awarded prior to 1914, 940 for the First World War, 40 between the wars and 380 from 1939–46.

29 h

Due to the vastly expanded nursing services called for by the First World War, a second class or Associate Royal Red Cross was introduced, and just over 5000 A.R.R.Cs were awarded. This compares with less than 1000 awarded for the Second World War.

| | | |
|---|---|---|
| | *1st Class* (R.R.C.) | |
| a | Victoria, gold and enamel | £500 |
| b | Victoria, silver gilt and enamel with gold centre | £150 |
| c | Edward VII, silver gilt and enamel | £250 |
| d | George V, silver gilt and enamel | £90 |
| e | George VI, silver gilt and enamel | £150 |
| f | E.IIR., silver gilt and enamel | £150 |
| g | Bars to the 1st class (including the original cross, Geo. V) | £250 |
| | *2nd Class* (A.R.R.C.) | |
| h | George V, silver and enamel | £45 |
| i | George VI, silver and enamel | £85 |
| j | E.IIR., silver and enamel | £60 |

## 30 The Distinguished Service Cross 1901

When first introduced in 1901, this was known as the Conspicuous Service Cross. The award was introduced as, in the opinion of the Admiralty, there was no suitable award for issue to junior officers who would hardly have been expected to qualify for the D.S.O. In 1914, at the outbreak of the First World War, the name of the decoration was altered to the Distinguished Service Cross, and in 1916 a second action bar was also introduced and, in 1931, the award was extended to the Merchant Navy and the Fishing Fleets. During the Second World War, the coverage of the Cross was even further extended so as to include RAF officers serving with the fleet as well as army officers serving aboard merchant ships, who were manning the defensive anti-aircraft and anti-submarine guns.

Only eight of the original C.S.Cs were awarded up to 1914, approximately 2000 D.S.Cs during the period 1914–18, 40 for the period 1920–38 and about 5000 for the Second World War, which reflects the more arduous part played by the navy in this war.

| | 1 *Unnamed Single* | 2 *General Citation* (*In a group with named medals**) | 3 *Average Citation* |
|---|---|---|---|
| a Edward VII | £1750 | £2000 | £2300 |
| b George V | £225 | £275 | £325 |
| c George VI | £275 | £325 | £400 |
| d George VI, 2nd type 'G.VIR.' | £450 | £525 | £625 |
| e E.IIR. | £500 | £600 | £725 |

*(* Value of other medals in group should be added)*

30 e

## 31 The Military Cross 1914

The Army, unlike the Royal Navy who possessed the Distinguished Service Cross, did not have a gallantry award for issue to the junior commissioned officers or warrant officers at the commencement of the 1914–18 war. The demands for such an award caused by the First World War made it very necessary to institute such an award, and the Military Cross was introduced on 28th December 1914.

In common with the other awards normally reserved for one branch of the services, the M.C. has been awarded to the Royal Navy and members of the RAF for services on the ground. The award is also available to Commonwealth and colonial forces. During the First World War over 40,000 Crosses were awarded which included 4 with as many as three bars. By comparison, during the Second World War only 11,000 were issued.

| | 1 *Unnamed Single* | 2 *General Citation* (*In a group with named medals**) | 3 *Average Citation* |
|---|---|---|---|
| a George V | £100 | £135 | £175 |
| b George V with bar | £165 | £220 | £275 |
| c George VI | £180 | £235 | £325 |
| d George VI, 2nd type 'G.VIR.' | £425 | £475 | £575 |
| e E.IIR. | £550 | £650 | £800 |

*(* Value of other medals in group should be added)*

31 a

## 32 The Distinguished Flying Cross 1918

Shortly after the Royal Air Force was formed on 1st April 1918, the Distinguished Flying Cross was introduced so as to recognize gallantry in active operations against the enemy. The award was made available to officers only; other ranks were issued with the Distinguished Flying Medal.

When the award was introduced, the riband was composed of violet and white horizontal stripes but, in common with the other three Air Force awards, the horizontal stripes were altered in July

32 33

1919 to diagonal stripes running at an angle of forty-five degrees. In 1941 the award was extended to the Fleet Air Arm serving with the RAF and from February 1942 it was also made available to personnel of the Dominions.

From the time it was instituted until the Second World War, comparatively few awards were made, namely just over 1200, while in the Second World War approximately 22,000 were awarded, whhch reflects the greatly enlarged force as well as six years of extremely extensive air activity. The award is occasionally given to the Navy and the Army, including a number of Army glider pilots for their services during the Second World War at Arnhem and elsewhere.

It follows that Crosses awarded for actions such as the Battle of Britain or for specific acts are more valuable and sought after than those sometimes awarded at the end of tours of active flying duty.

| | | | *In a group with named medals** | |
|---|---|---|---|---|
| | | 1 *Unnamed Single* | 2 *General Citation* | 3 *Average Citation* |
| a | George V | £375 | £450 | £525 |
| b | George VI | £200 | £250 | £325 |
| c | George VI, 2nd type 'G.VIR.' | £475 | £550 | £600 |
| d | E.IIR. | £550 | £625 | £675 |

*(* Value of other medals in group should be added)*

## 33 Air Force Cross 1918

This award was instituted in June 1918 at the same time as the D.F.C., D.F.M. and A.F.M. thus completing the series of four available to the RAF. The Air Force Cross is awarded for the same type of actions as the Air Force Medal, the Cross being reserved for officers. The role of the A.F.C. was to reward those who had distinguished themselves in the air, though *not* in active operations against the enemy, although it follows that those in the Air Force were constantly risking their lives undertaking not only experimental work but day to day training, navigational and flying exercises.

As with the other three Air Force awards, the first riband issued comprised horizontal red and white stripes, but shortly afterwards these were superseded by diagonal stripes.

Up until the Second World War, just over 850 were issued, including 12 first bars and 3 with second bars. During the Second World War, just over 2000 were awarded and since 1945, again just over 2000, which probably reflects the increased danger and risk in testing and generally flying the more modern aircraft. Typical of the reasons for award were those to Ft Lt Adam for an altitude record of 52,936ft in 1938 and to the Duke of Hamilton, who in 1934 was the first man to fly over Mount Everest.

| | 1 *Unnamed Single* | 2 *In a Named Group with average citation details** |
|---|---|---|
| a George V | £350 | £425 |
| b George VI | £250 | £300 |
| c George VI, 2nd type 'G.VIR.' | £300 | £400 |
| d E.IIR. | £300 | £400 |

*(* Value of other medals in groups should be added)*

## 34 The Order of British India 1837

This award was introduced by the Honourable East India Company in 1837 to reward its Indian officers for outstanding, long and meritorious service. The Order consists of two classes, both of them in gold with enamelled centres which were worn around the neck from a crimson riband that was originally sky blue. The sky-blue riband was changed as it was not found to be pratical, owing to the habit among all classes of natives of oiling their hair, which naturally soiled the riband.

An interesting aspect of this award is that, after the partition of India and Pakistan in 1946, the Pakistan Government ordered a quantity from the London medallists Spink & Son Ltd for award

34 b

to *British* officers who had rendered outstanding services to Pakistan. These contained a pale blue enamel centre (from 1939) and border. The donors and recipients of the award were thus completely reversed.

| | | |
|---|---|---|
| a | 1st class (gold) light blue centre with dark blue garter surrounding | £600 |
| b | 1st class (gold) light blue centre and garter (Introduced 1939) | £650 |
| c | 2nd class in gold (without crown) | £275 |

## 35 The Order of Burma 1940

Established by George VI in 1940 at the same time as the Burma Gallantry Medal. For administration purposes, Burma became independent of the Indian subcontinent in 1937 and, as a result, separate awards had to be introduced. The Order of Burma was awarded in very limited numbers to the Burma Army, the Burma Frontier Force and the Burma Military Police for long, faithful and honourable service. The award was abolished in 1947.

£3750

36 c & d

## 36 The Kaiser-i-Hind Medal 1900

Introduced by Queen Victoria in 1900 for award to those irrespective of nationality, colour, creed or sex who had performed useful public service in India, it was frequently given for social work and similar services.

The decoration was issued in both gold and silver, and bronze medals were also introduced for issue during the reign of George V. It was abolished in 1947 upon the partition of the Indian subcontinent. When awarded to service personnel or gentlemen, the decoration is worn in the same way as a service medal, when worn by a lady on evening dress, the badge is then suspended on a riband and fashioned into a bow. Issued unnamed.

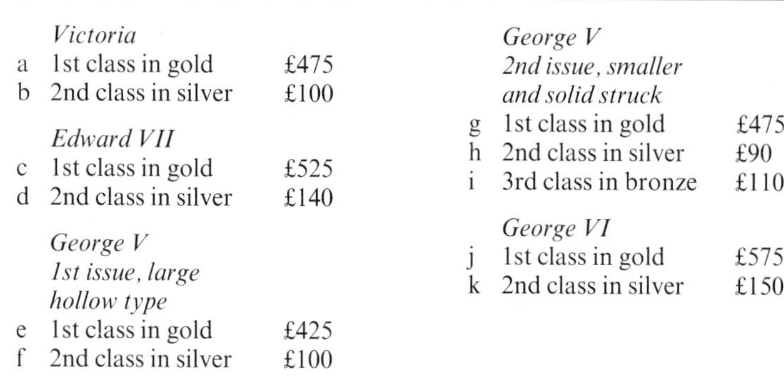

| | | |
|---|---|---|
| | *Victoria* | |
| a | 1st class in gold | £475 |
| b | 2nd class in silver | £100 |
| | *Edward VII* | |
| c | 1st class in gold | £525 |
| d | 2nd class in silver | £140 |
| | *George V 1st issue, large hollow type* | |
| e | 1st class in gold | £425 |
| f | 2nd class in silver | £100 |
| | *George V 2nd issue, smaller and solid struck* | |
| g | 1st class in gold | £475 |
| h | 2nd class in silver | £90 |
| i | 3rd class in bronze | £110 |
| | *George VI* | |
| j | 1st class in gold | £575 |
| k | 2nd class in silver | £150 |

37 a

## 37 The Albert Medal 1866

The Albert Medal was originally instituted in 1866 as a one-class award, but the royal warrant was then amended a year later so as to include two classes—a first class and a second class. The award was originally introduced to recognize distinguished acts of gallantry at sea, and some ten years later, in 1877, the award was extended to acts of gallantry in saving life on land. The wording around the perimeter of the two types of decoration indicates whether the action was at sea or on land. In addition, the riband awarded for the sea issues is blue and white, while that for land is red and white, with the enamelling in the centre matching the red or blue.

The Albert Medal was named after Prince Albert, the Prince Consort, who died in 1861; the general esteem that this award quickly gained earned it the unofficial name of 'the civilian V.C.'. Like the V.C. the decoration entitled one to a gratuity irrespective of class, and in 1968 this was £100. In 1949 the first class was abolished in favour of the George Cross, and more recently all those entitled to the second class have had the decoration changed, again for the George Cross. The youngest recipients were Antony Fraser, aged eight and Dorothy Ashburn aged eleven, who saved each other's lives when attacked by a cougar in Canada, and also David Weston, aged ten, who attempted to save the lives of three companions who had fallen through the ice of a frozen lake. The numbers issued which are shown in brackets below indicate how few awards were issued in the space of some one hundred years.

| | | 1 *Civilians* | 2 *Armed Forces* |
|---|---|---|---|
| a | Albert Medal in gold for gallantry in saving life at sea (1st class) (25) | £1500 | £2000 |
| b | Albert Medal in bronze for gallantry in saving life at sea (2nd class) (216) | £725 | £800 |
| c | Albert Medal in gold for gallantry in saving life on land (1st class) (45) | £1300 | £1700 |
| d | Albert Medal in bronze for gallantry in saving life on land (2nd class) (282) | £650 | £725 |

## 38 The King's (later Queen's) Medal for Bravery (South Africa) 1939

38

Introduced in 1939 to reward acts of life-saving within the Union of South Africa or in territories administered by the Union. Two classes were introduced, the first being in gold which has only been awarded on one occasion, the second class in silver, which has been awarded on thirty-five occasions. The award was abolished upon South Africa becoming a republic and was replaced by the Woltemade Decoration for Bravery, the conditions of which are similar to the cancelled Queen's Medal.

a Gold £4500 b Silver (Geo. VI issue) £600

## 39 The Distinguished Conduct Medal

39

Prior to the Crimean War, there were no official gallantry medals for other ranks of the British Army, although some regiments did issue unofficial gallantry medals at their own expense, which were invariably individually engraved.

It was the Crimean War which caused the D.C.M. to be instituted for other ranks only. Before 1894 the award was available to dominion and colonial forces, but after this date, each of the different countries had its own award, which invariably contained a distinctive title on the reverse.

Very few awards were given for some of the campaigns, which is illustrated by the price structure for the medals awarded for the various wars or campaigns as given below. Additional awards are represented by a bar attached to the riband—11 medals were awarded with *two* bars representing three awards. The first type of bar introduced in 1881 contained the date of the action in relief lettering, the present-day second action laurel bar was introduced in 1916. As with other service awards, the D.C.M. has been given to the Navy, principally to the RNVR battalions, who served on the Western Front throughout a considerable part of the First World War.

| | | |
|---|---|---|
| a | Victoria | |
| 1 | Crimea (750), Heavy Bde | £550 |
| 2 | Light Bde | £1000 |
| 3 | General | £300 |
| 4 | Mutiny (9) | £2000 |
| 5 | I.G.S. 1854–94 period/area | £750 |
| 6 | Abyssinia 1868 (7) | £2000 |
| 7 | Ashantee 1873–74 (33) | £1000 |
| 8 | S. Africa 1877–79 (15) | £1750 |
| 9 | Afghanistan 1878–80 (61) | £450 |
| 10 | Egypt 1882 (135) | £350 |
| 11 | I.G.S. 1895–1901 | £300 |
| 12 | Sudan 1896–97 | £450 |
| 13 | S. Africa 1899–1902 (2050) | £250 |
| b | Edward VII | £200 |
| c | George V, uncrowned head (1914–18 War etc) (25,000) | £100 |
| d | George V, uncrowned head (1914–18 War etc) to R.N.V.R. Bns | £450 |
| e | George V and 2nd action bar | £225 |
| f | George V, crowned head (1930–37) (14) | £1400 |
| g | George VI 'Indiae Imp' legend (1937–47) | £200 |
| h | George VI 'Indiae Imp' deleted 1948– | £625 |
| i | E.IIR. 'D.G.BR:OMN:REGINA F:D.' legend | £450 |
| j | E.IIR. 'DEI. GRATIA REGINA F.D.' legend | £650 |
| | COLONIAL ISSUES | |
| k | **Canada**, Victoria | £2500 |
| | **Natal & Cape of Good Hope** | |
| l | Victoria | *Rare* |
| m | Edward VII | £1850 |
| | **New Zealand** | |
| n | (10 were purchased by the authorities in 1898, examples are known to be in collections. Specimens have probably been on the market.) | £2000 |
| | **Royal West African Frontier Force** | |
| o | Edward VII £375 | |
| p | George V | £275 |
| | **King's African Rifles** | |
| q | Edward VII £475 | |
| r | George V | £275 |

40

## 40 The Conspicuous Gallantry Medal (Royal Navy 1855 and Royal Air Force 1943)

The Naval medal had two different reverses, the first medal being introduced in 1855 for award during the war against Russia. This medal was virtually the same as the Meritorious Service Medal, with the die-struck wording on the reverse, 'Meritorious Service' being erased and 'Conspicuous Gallantry' engraved. The first die-struck word 'For' remained.

The award of the medal lapsed at the end of the Crimean War and it was then instituted on a more permanent basis in 1874, following the successful conclusion of the Ashantee war 1873–74. At that time a special die was introduced so that the medal was awarded with normal relief wording, reading 'For Conspicious Gallantry'. Only twelve of the original Crimean period awards were issued to eleven recipients (one recipient twice). Since 1874 the decoration has been given very sparingly, only 235 being given in all, including 108 for the First World War, 72 for the Second World War, and 1 for the recent Falkland Islands conflict.

During the Second World War, it was realized that the Distinguished Flying Medal was not sufficient to cover the deeds performed by NCOs and men of the RAF. Consequently, the C.G.M. was extended to the RAF, this being senior to the existing D.F.M. The RAF award is the same as the Naval medal in all respects except that it is worn with a light blue riband with dark blue edges as opposed to the Naval white with dark blue edges. From 1943–45 only 109 awards were given which were very few when one considers the vastly enlarged Royal Air Force at that time. Between 1946 and 1979 only one medal was awarded, this was in 1968 to the Royal Australian Air Force for Vietnam.

| | | | | | |
|---|---|---|---|---|---|
| a | Victoria | £1200 | d | George VI | £1200 |
| b | Edward VII | £3500 | e | E.IIR. *None awarded* | —— |
| c | George VI | £950 | | | |
| **C.G.M. (Royal Air Force 1943)** | | | | | |
| f | George VI | £1000 | g | E.IIR. (1 only awarded) | £4000 |

41

## 41 The George Medal 1940

Instituted at the same time as the George Cross, this was intended primarily for civilians and military services, in the latter case being confined to actions where purely military honours are not normally granted. Very many more George Medals have been awarded than George Crosses, in fact the total is just under 2000, most of these being for the wartime period 1940–45. Bars are awarded to commemorate a second action, twenty-five having been awarded to date.

| | | | | | |
|---|---|---|---|---|---|
| 1 | Service awards | | 2 | Civilian awards | |
| a | Geo. VI | £650 | c | Geo. VI | £500 |
| b | E.IIR. | £950 | d | E.IIR. | £800 |

## 42 The King's Police Medal, The King's Police and Fire Brigades Medal 1909 The Queen's Police Medal and the Queen's Fire Service Medal 1954

Originally introduced by King Edward VII in 1909 for rewarding the police forces and fire brigades of Great Britain and the dominions. Prior to 1933, the awards were all general issues, but from 1933 onwards, two reverses were issued, one reading 'For Gallantry' and the other reading 'For Distinguished Service'. Those issued with the effigy of Edward VII are scarce and in no period can they be regarded as common.

In 1937 a special design of the King's Police Medal was introduced solely for South Africa, the reverse of the Gallantry Medal reading 'For Bravery' and *'Africaan Vir Dapperheid'* and that 'For Distinguished Service' also had *'Vir Voortreflike Diens'* on the reverse. Some thirty awards were given for gallantry and seventeen for distinguished service in connection with South Africa.

42a

The Queen's Police Medal is quite a recent award, having been approved by Her Majesty on 19th May 1954. Prior to 1954, the fire brigades were eligible for the King's Police and Fire Brigades Medal. The Queen's Fire Service Medal is issued with one of two only) and the other 'For Distinguished Fire Service'. To date, less reverses, one reading 'For Gallantry' (awarded posthumously than forty awards have been made for gallantry, while about 2000 awards have been made for distinguished service. Recipients are allowed to use the post nominal letters Q.P.M.

The Queen's Fire Service Medal was introduced in 1954, it being considered desirable to have a separate medal for the fire brigade as opposed to the combined Police and Fire Brigades Medal. As with the Queen's Police Medal, two different issues were introduced, one reverse being for gallantry and the other for distinguished service. Fewer than 500 Distinguished Service Medals have been awarded to date, and it is believed there have been no awards for gallantry. In 1969 Her Majesty approved of the use by recipients of the post nominal letters Q.F.S.M.

| | | | |
|---|---|---|---|
| a | *Pre–1933 General Issues* | | |
| | 1 Edward VII £400 | | 2 George V £125 |
| b | *Post–1933 for Distinguished Service* | | |
| | 1 George V £325 | 2 George VI £225 | 3 E.IIR. £175 |
| c | *Post–1933 for Gallantry* | | |
| | 1 George V £400 | 2 George VI £250 | 3 E.II.R. £600 |
| d | *South African Issue* | | |
| | For Gallantry | | |
| | 1 George VI £600 | | 2 E.IIR. £350 |
| | For Distinguished Service | | |
| | 3 George V £350 | | 4 George VI £750 |

## 43 The Edward Medal 1907

Introduced in 1907 as, prior to this date, the only available decoration for civilians was the Albert Medal which was only sparingly granted. When the medal was first suggested, its object was to reward acts of gallantry in mines and quarries, but within a year or two it was extended to include a second issue for industry generally. Two different types of reverses were issued, and both medals were in silver and bronze.

When the George Cross and George Medal were introduced in 1940, awards for civilian acts of courage and devotion became confusing. Consequently, in 1949, King George VI decreed that the silver Edward Medal should cease and that all future bronze medals should be awarded posthumously.

The scarcest type is the industrial issue in silver; only twenty-five were awarded as opposed to seventy-seven for miners. As from 1968, surviving UK recipients of the Edward Medals were entitled to annual gratuities of £100, irrespective if their award was a silver or a bronze medal. The medal was eventually entirely abolished in 1971 and recipients living at that time were deemed to have been awarded the George Cross; accordingly, the medals were, or could have been, exchanged with a Cross.

| | *Miner's Issue* | 1 *Silver* | 2 *Bronze* |
|---|---|---|---|
| a | Edward VII | £550 | £300 |
| b | George V | £500 | £140 |
| c | George VI | £600 | £450 |
| d | E.IIR. | *None awarded* | £700 |
| | *Industrial Issue* | | |
| e | Edward VII | £900 | £650 |
| f | George V | £300 | £150 |
| g | George VI | £800 | £375 |
| h | E.IIR. | £1200 | £500 |

## 44 The Indian Distinguished Service Medal 1907

Introduced in 1907 as an award to recognize the distinguished services of Indian commissioned and non-commissioned officers, and also men of the regular land forces in India. Later, in 1929, the award was extended to the Indian Marines and in 1940 to the Indian Air Force. In 1944 it was extended yet again to include the Hong Kong and Singapore Royal Artillery. Just over 5300 awards were made, including some 50 second action bars, between 1907 and 1947 when the medal was abolished following the granting of independence to India and Pakistan. The majority, just over 3000, were awarded during the First World War and almost 1150 during the Second World War.

| | | |
|---|---|---|
| a | Edward VII | £350 |
| b | George V, 1st type, 'Kaiser-I-Hind' | £100 |
| c | George V, 2nd type | £225 |
| d | George VI | £125 |

## 45 The Burma Gallantry Medal 1940

Burma, having ceased to be part of British India for administration purposes in 1937, caused this silver medal to be introduced in 1940. The award ceased in 1947 when Burma was granted independence. During its lifetime, just over 200 awards were made, including 3 second award bars. The gallantry medal was conferred by the Governor of Burma upon the officers and non-commissioned officers and other ranks of the Burma Army, the Frontier Force, the Military Police, the Burma Royal Naval Volunteer Reserve and the Auxiliary Air Force for acts of conspicuous gallantry performed in connection with their duties.

£500

## 46 The Distinguished Service Medal

This is another gallantry award introduced as a result of the demands caused by the First World War. It was intended to supplement the Conspicuous Gallantry Medal and to be the other ranks' counterpart to the Distinguished Service Cross. A bar was approved in 1916 to be awarded as a second action bar. Like other service decorations, the award of the medal was extended during the Second World War to cover Army and RAF personnel serving aboard ships and was also extended to include the Merchant Navies of Britain and the Commonwealth.

During the First World War, approximately 5600 were awarded, including 2 with second award bars, while during the Second

46

World War just under 7300 were issued, including one with as many as three bars. Naturally, those awarded for the outstanding actions of the First and Second World Wars command higher prices, such as Jutland, the Falkland Islands (1914–18 period) Zeebrugge and, in the Second World War, the destruction of the German super battleship the Scharnhorst, etc, as well as the post-war period in for instance Korea and for Yangtze.

| | 1 *General Citation* | 2 *Average Citation* |
|---|---|---|
| a George V, 1st type, uncrowned head (1914–30) | £150 | £200 |
| b George V, 2nd type, crowned head (1930–37) | £800 | £900 |
| c George VI, 1st type, with 'Ind.Imp' in legend (1938–49) | £200 | £225 |
| d George VI, 2nd type, without 'Ind.Imp' in legend (1949–53) | £600 | £675 |
| e E.IIR., 1st type, with 'Br.Omn' in legend (153–57) | £700 | £800 |
| f E.IHR., 2nd type, without 'Br.Omn' in legend (1957– ) | £650 | £700 |

*For details of recipients, see* The Distinguished Service Medal 1914–20 *and* 1939–46, *both volumes available from Spink & Son Ltd.*

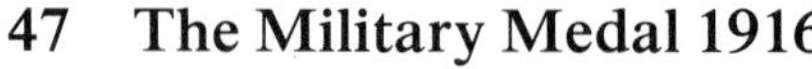

## 47 The Military Medal 1916

47 a–d

This again was introduced during the First World War, rather late on, namely March 1916, for award to NCOs and men for individual or even associated acts of bravery in the field. In June of that year, it was also extended to women. The award is junior to the Distinguished Conduct Medal, consequently rather more have been issued, in fact it is recognized that this is probably the most common of the British gallantry awards. Over 120,000 were awarded for the First World War and yet, as a contrast, just under 16,000 were issued for the rather longer Second World War. The First World War issues no doubt reflected the appalling close combat conditions and battles that lasted for the four years of the war.

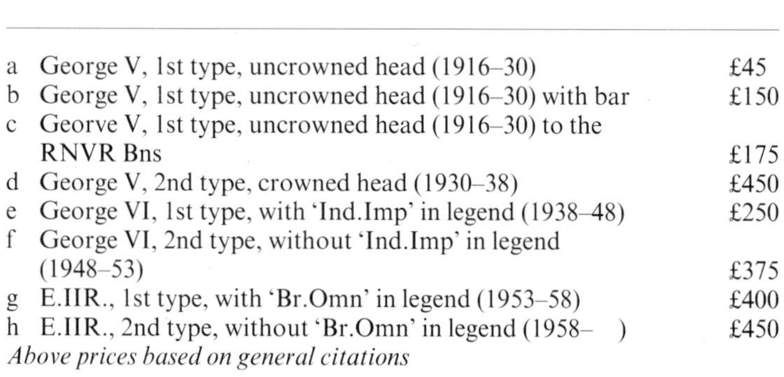
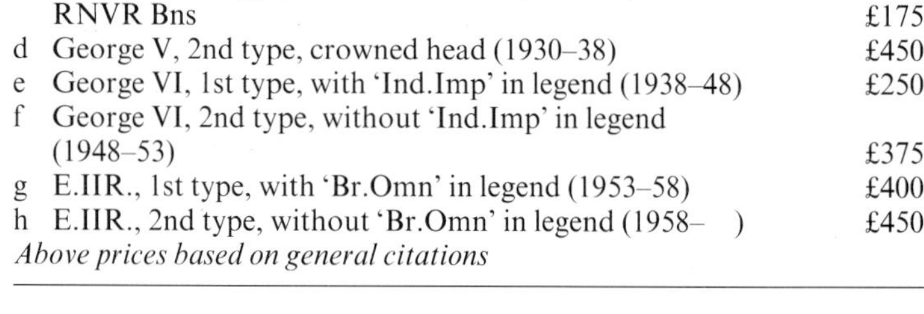

| | |
|---|---|
| a George V, 1st type, uncrowned head (1916–30) | £45 |
| b George V, 1st type, uncrowned head (1916–30) with bar | £150 |
| c Georve V, 1st type, uncrowned head (1916–30) to the RNVR Bns | £175 |
| d George V, 2nd type, crowned head (1930–38) | £450 |
| e George VI, 1st type, with 'Ind.Imp' in legend (1938–48) | £250 |
| f George VI, 2nd type, without 'Ind.Imp' in legend (1948–53) | £375 |
| g E.IIR., 1st type, with 'Br.Omn' in legend (1953–58) | £400 |
| h E.IIR., 2nd type, without 'Br.Omn' in legend (1958– ) | £450 |

*Above prices based on general citations*

## 48 The Distinguished Flying Medal 1918

This was introduced at the same time and for the same reasons as the Distinguished Flying Cross. The medal was made available to NCO aircrew and men (officers received the Distinguished Flying cross) for acts of valour, courage or devotion to duty while flying on active operations against the enemy.

Having been introduced as late as April 1918, few awards were issued for the First World War, in fact only about 100 issues were made. Between the two World Wars, a further 80 were issued with 2 first-award bars. The Second World War saw a vastly increased Air Force; this called for the issue of just over 6500 D.F.Ms, 60 first-award bars and 1 second bar.

| | | |
|---|---|---|
| a | George V, 1st type, uncrowned head (1918–30) | £750 |
| b | George V, 2nd type, crowned head (1930–38) | £950 |
| c | George VI, 1st type, with 'Ind.Imp' in legend (1938–49) | £300 |
| d | George VI, 2nd type, without 'Ind.Imp' in legend (1949–53) | £600 |
| e | E.IIR. | £525 |

*Above prices based on general citations*

## 49 The Air Force Medal 1918

This was approved on 3rd January 1918 shortly after the formation of the Royal Air Force. It was intended for award to NCOs and men (officers received the Air Force Cross) and was awarded for acts of valour, courage or devotion to duty performed while flying, though *not* on active operations against the enemy. Far fewer Air Force Medals were awarded than the Distinguished Flying Medal, some 850 being awarded since its institution plus 9 second action bars. Originally, when the medal was authorized, it had a riband with horizontal stripes of red and white but this was altered to diagonal stripes in July 1919. In August 1919 the regulations were altered so that the award could be given to individuals of other services or even civilians who rendered distinguished service to aviation in actual flying. The award is much scarcer than the Distinguished Flying Medal but nevertheless is not perhaps quite as appealing to collectors who much prefer awards issued for service in the face of the enemy.

| | | |
|---|---|---|
| a | George V, 1st type, uncrowned head (1918–30) | £600 |
| b | George V, 2nd type, crowned head (1930–38) | £750 |
| c | George VI, 1st type, with 'Ind.Imp' in legend (1938–49) | £375 |
| d | George VI, 2nd type, without 'Ind.Imp' in legend (1949–53) | £450 |
| e | E.IIR. | £425 |

## 50 The Indian Police and Fire Brigades Medal 1932

Instituted in 1932 as a reward for the Indian police forces and the Indian fire brigades for services of conspicuous merit. The King's Police Medal was available but this was restricted to fifty awards for the Indian forces. After 1944 two different types of the Indian Police Medal were issued, one read 'For Gallantry' and the other 'For Meritorious Service'. Prior to 1944, one common reverse had been used, which read 'For Distinguished Conduct'. The medals, always in bronze, continued to be awarded after the creation of the Dominion of India in 1947, but ceased when India became a republic in 1950.

| | | |
|---|---|---|
| a | George V, common reverse 'For Distinguished Conduct' | £175 |
| b | George VI, common reverse 'For Distinguished Conduct' | £250 |
| c | George VI, reverse 'For Gallantry' (1945) | £450 |
| d | George VI, reverse 'For Meritorious Service' (1945) | £250 |

## 51 The Burma Police Medal 1937

Burma was made independent of India in 1937 when Burma became a separate colony. It was then found necessary to introduce a gallantry award which was given to the police forces in addition to the fire brigades. The maximum number that could be awarded in any one year was twenty-five. The award was in bronze and carried the effigy of George VI with a legend on the reverse reading 'Burma Police, for Distinguished Conduct'. In addition to being awarded for distinguished conduct, it was also awarded for long service where the recipient had shown ability and merit. From 1937 until after the Second World War when Burma became independent, there were approximately 140 awards made. The decoration was given to both European and Burmese recipients.

| | | |
|---|---|---|
| a | If awarded for Gallantry | £275 |
| b | If awarded for Meritorious Service | £175 |

## 52 The Colonial Police and Fire Brigades Medals for Gallantry and Meritorious Service 1938

These medals for the two services were introduced in May 1938 as a reward for distinguished conduct, in the colonies and territories administered by the UK. The medal contained the usual Sovereign's effigy on the obverse, while the reverse contained either (a) a police truncheon and wreath surrounded by 'Colonial Police Forces for Gallantry' or (b) a fireman's helmet, axe and wreath and surrounding 'Colonial Fire Brigade for Gallantry'. The medals and ribands are the same as the Colonial Meritorious Service Medals, but the riband has an additional red stripe in the centre. The medals awarded to the fire brigades are very much rarer than those to the police, the ratio being about 1:38. To date, no awards have been made to women.

| | | 1 *Police* | 2 *Fire* |
|---|---|---|---|
| | *George VI* | | |
| a | For Gallantry | £250 | £650 |
| b | For Meritorious Service | £125 | £400 |
| | *E.IIR.* | | |
| c | For Gallantry | £300 | £400 |
| d | For Meritorious Service | £70 | £175 |

53

## 53 The Queen's Gallantry Medal 1974

Introduced as recently as June 1974 to reward recognized acts of gallantry of a slightly lower degree than that normally required for the George Cross and the George Medal. Prior to the introduction of the Queen's Gallantry Medal, the Order of the British Empire was frequently awarded. The award is made available to all civilians and service personnel both in the UK and overseas territories, the medal being intended primarily for actions for which purely military honours are not normally granted. Recipients are allowed to use the post nominal letters Q.G.M. after their name. Since being introduced, less than 400 awards have been issued.

a Services £400 b Civilians £200

## 54 The Allied Subjects Medal

This is really a 'service' medal as opposed to a gallantry medal, and was awarded in silver and bronze to both men and women for assistance to British soldiers behind the enemy's lines. Although this is really a service medal, it has been included here as many recipients risked the lives of themselves and their families.

One hundred and thirty-four silver medals 574 bronze medals were issued, the majority going to Belgian and French nationals.

---

a Silver (104) £850 b Bronze (525) £400

---

## 55 The King's Medal for Courage in the Cause of Freedom 1947

This was the Second World War's counterpart to the Allied Subjects Medal awarded during the First World War. However, during the Second World War, two medals were given, one for *courage* in the cause of freedom and the other for *service* in the cause of freedom. The courage medal was awarded to foreign civilians and members of foreign armed forces in respect of special services such as clandestine operations, which were outside the scope of normal military duties, in furtherance of the interest of the British Commonwealth in the Allied cause during the war. Approximately 3200 medals for courage were awarded, the issues taking place in 1947.

---

(3,200) £300

---

## 56 The Sea Gallantry Medal 1854

The medal originated through the Merchant Shipping Act of 1854, and is the only gallantry medal instituted by an act of Parliament. The medal was originally rather oversized, being 2.25in in diameter, and was not intended for wear with a riband. However, after 1902 Edward VII, who began to take a personal interest in the award and to present some of them himself, decreed that the size was to be reduced to 1.25in in diameter and was to be worn with a riband as modern-day medals. Originally, there were two different types of obverse, which were discontinued in 1893, one read 'Awarded by the Board of Trade for Gallantry in Saving Life' and the other read 'Awarded by the Board of Trade for Saving Life at Sea'. The 'Gallantry' medal was awarded for those who actually

56

56

risked their lives in acts of saving life, while the other medal, 'for Saving Life at Sea', was awarded to people who provided back-up services, such as a captain of a ship. The latter was known as the Humanity Medal and was awarded rather infrequently. There were almost 500 of the original large silver medals issued and some 750 bronze. Regarding the smaller modern issues, almost 500 each of the silver and bronze were awarded. As a matter of interest, only 1 second action bar was awarded, this being presented to Chief Officer James Whitely.

| | | 1 *Silver* | 2 *Bronze* |
|---|---|---|---|
| a | Original 2.25in medal for gallantry | £275 | £185 |
| b | Original 2.25in medal for Humanity | £225 | £140 |
| c | Edward VII, 1st issue | £600 | £400 |
| d | Edward VII, 2nd issue ('Awarded by the Board of Trade' deleted from obverse) | £175 | £100 |
| e | George V | £110 | £90 |
| f | George VI, 1st issue | £250 | £175 |
| g | George VI, 2nd issue, 'G.VIR.' legend *None Awarded* | —— | £325 |
| h | E.IIR. | £225 | £300 |

## 57 The Sea Gallantry Medal (Foreign Services) 1841

This medal was approved by Queen Victoria in 1841 to recognize the services of foreigners to British subjects and was awarded in gold, silver and bronze. Originally, a special reverse was struck for each occasion, but it was found that this was an unnecessary expense and in 1849 two standard reverses were introduced, 'For Saving the Life of a British Subject' and 'For assisting a British vessel in distress'. The medal as originally issued was 1.85in in diameter, but was reduced in size to 1.25in in 1854.

| | | Large medals to 1854 | | | Small medals from 1854 | |
|---|---|---|---|---|---|---|
| | | 1 *Gold* | 2 *Silver* | 3 *Bronze* | 4 *Gold* | 5 *Silver* |
| a | Victoria | £850 | £150 | £175 | £400 | £70 |
| b | Edward VII | —— | —— | —— | £850 | £350 |
| c | George V | —— | —— | —— | £600 | £140 |
| d | George VI | —— | —— | —— | —— | £350 |
| e | E.IIR. | —— | —— | —— | £950 | £350 |

57

# Campaign Medals

*Readers are recommended to study the 5th edition of* British Battles & Medals *by Major L. L. Gordon, revised by E. C. Joslin, published by Spink & Son Ltd., for a comprehensive study of campaign medals.*

*It must be understood that a number of the earlier campaign medals (Nos 58 to 78 inclusive) were privately struck and in some cases later strikings have been made;* **the prices given are based on original strikings**. *These were always issued unnamed, which is the basis used here for values.*

## The Honourable East India Company's Medals 1778–1837 and early privately issued Campaign Medals (Nos. 58–79)

The Honourable East India Company was an association of merchant venturers formed in London in 1599. They formed the Company for the purpose of trading with the Far East and later assumed considerable power. The gigantic power that the Company wielded until just after the Indian Mutiny (1856–57) made it necessary for them to maintain a considerable army and navy to guard not only its immediate local possessions and factories, but also to ensure continued safety by enlarging its territories until it reached a stage where the Company was controlling most of the Indian subcontinent. This in turn brought the Company frequently into conflict with neighbouring states and in addition it also had to contest territories claimed by the French and other nations.

We are indebted to the HEIC, as it is normally known, for setting the example of issuing campaign or service medals long before the British Government's general issue to officers and men alike, namely for Waterloo in 1815.

The early medals, except for Burma 1824–26 were often of two sizes, sometimes in gold and silver with very simple ring suspenders and without standard ribands as we know them today. Furthermore, they were issued unnamed; consequently, these earlier medals are listed separately.

In addition to the HEIC, a number of private individuals and associations issued medals at their own expense; after the introduction of the official Government medal for Waterloo, private medals lapsed.

58

## 58 The Louisbourg Medal 1758

This was in the nature of a gallantry or distinguished service medal being conferred on selected recipients only, who took part in the capture of Louisbourg in Canada from the French on 27th July 1758. Generals Amhurst and Wolfe commanded the land forces and Admiral Boscawen the fleet.

| a Gold (4 known) | £8500 | b Silver | £1100 | c Bronze | £425 |
|---|---|---|---|---|---|

## 59 The Carib War Medal 1773

Silver medals were awarded by the Legislative Assembly of the island of St Vincent to the Militia or Volunteers who had taken part in the campaign against the Caribs or natives of the Island who had been encouraged to rebel against the English by the French settlers.

£950

## 60 The Deccan Medal 1778–84

These medals were struck in Calcutta and were either 1.6in or 1.25in in diameter; the larger size, a few of which were in gold, were issued to officers only. This was the first of the Company's general issue of medals, awarded for services in Western India and Gujerat, under the overall leadership of Warren Hastings.

The reverse contains a Persian inscription which, translated, reads: 'As coins are current in the world, so shall be the bravery and exploits of those heroes by whom the name of the victorious English nation was carried from Bengal to the Deccan. Presented in AD 1784 [Hegira 1199] by the East India Company's Calcutta Government.'

| | 1 *Gold* | 2 *Silver* |
|---|---|---|
| a 1.6in dia. | £1850 | £500 |
| b 1.25in dia. | (*Not issued*) | £200 |

61 b

## 61 The Defence of Gibraltar Medals 1779–83

The two most common medals awarded for the defence of Gibraltar are the silver ones presented to officers by Generals Picton and Eliott at their own expense. There were, however, other medals given for the same event. The Defence of Gibraltar was carried out by some 7000 British and Hanoverian troops against the combined forces of Spain and France, the French having some 40,000 troops in the initial assault.

| | |
|---|---|
| a General Picton's Medal, silver | £300 |
| b General Eliott's Medal, silver | £225 |

## 62 The Mysore Campaign Medal 1790–92

Produced in two sizes, 1.5in and 1.7in in diameter, the larger was awarded in gold and silver, the smaller in silver only. The medals were awarded to the officers and men employed by the H.E.I. Company under the leadership of Lord Cornwallis and Generals Meadows and Abercrombie, for the defeat of the powerful Tippoo

Sahib, ruler of Mysore.

| | 1 *Gold* | 2 *Silver* |
|---|---|---|
| a 1.7in dia. | £1750 | £350 |
| b 1.5in dia. | (*Not issued*) | £200 |

## 63 The capture of Ceylon Medal 1795

This was awarded for services during the capture of the island of Ceylon from the Dutch, the campaign resulting from the Napoleonic Wars.

Two medals were awarded in gold to Captains Baden and Clarke and approximately 121 in silver to native gunners of the Bengal Artillery.

| | | | |
|---|---|---|---|
| a Gold (2) | £8000 | b Silver (120) | £575 |

63

## 64 The Isle of St Vincent Medal 1795

The issue of this bronze medal came about due to circumstances which were similar to those in 1773, which were commemorated by the Carib War Medal. Awarded to the officers and NCOs of the Corps of Natives which numbered 500 men, which was raised by Major Seton from among the slaves, the medal is often referred to as 'St Vincent's Black Corps Medal'.

The campaign was against the Caribs or natives and French troops.

£100

64

## 65 The Davison's Nile Medal 1798

This medal was a personal award by Nelson's price agent—a Mr Davison—to all the officers and men present. The admirals and captains were awarded the medal in gold which is, of course, very scarce. Other officers received silver medals, while petty officers were given gold-plated bronze medals and the remainder were issued with bronze medals. The reverse shows an interesting pictorial scene of the fleet in Aboukir Bay with an inscription. The official Government medals for the Nile were not issued for another fifty years and then they were only issued to the survivors living at that time.

| | | | |
|---|---|---|---|
| a Gold | £3250 | b Bronze gilt | £120 |
| c Silver | £150 | d Bronze | £80 |

65

## 66 The Seringapatam Medal 1799

Tippoo Sahib, ruler of Mysore, who had been defeated during the campaign 1790–92, was attacked by the Company's forces due to his hostile movements and his negotiations with the French. The medals were awarded to both British and Indian regiments for the capture of the fortress of Seringapatam on the 4th May. The left wing of the forces was under the command of Lt-Col the Honourable Arthur Wellesley, later the Duke of Wellington, this being one of the actions which later gained him the nickname of 'The Sepoy General'. The Company took over the administration

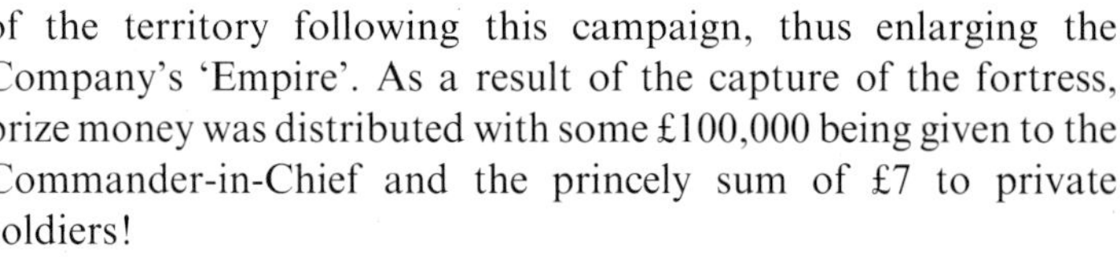

of the territory following this campaign, thus enlarging the Company's 'Empire'. As a result of the capture of the fortress, prize money was distributed with some £100,000 being given to the Commander-in-Chief and the princely sum of £7 to private soldiers!

The medals, struck in England were 1.9in in diameter and those in Calcutta 1.8in in diameter. They were struck in gold, silver gilt, silver, bronze and pewter, although the smaller 1.8in was produced in gold and silver only.

66

| | 1 *Gold* (113) | 2 *Silver Gilt* (185) | 3 *Silver* (3600) | 4 *Bronze* (5000) | 5 *Pewter* (45,000) |
|---|---|---|---|---|---|
| a 1.9in | £1850 | £375 | £200 | £120 | £80 |
| b 1.8in | £950 | (*Not issued*) | £175 | (*Not issued*) | (*Not issued*) |

## 67 The Earl St Vincent's Medal 1800

67

Awarded by Admiral Earl St Vincent to the crew of his ship HMS *Ville de Paris* who remained loyal during the mutiny of the fleet in the Mediterranean, which followed the infamous mutiny of the home fleet anchored off The Nore in 1797. Awarded in silver, although it is thought that a few gold specimens were presented to selected people holding high office.

| a Gold | £4750 | b Silver | £220 |
|---|---|---|---|

## Egypt 1801
## 68 The Honourable East India Company's Medal

Medals were issued by the Hon. East India Company to both the British and Indian regiments that had set out from India to assist the troops from the UK during their capture of Egypt, which had been occupied by Napoleon's troops. An expedition to conquer the country was despatched from England under General Abercrombie, and additional forces were sent from India and also the Cape of Good Hope, under the command of General Baird. Sixteen medals were issued in gold and 2200 in silver, the medals being 1.9in in diameter. In addition, the Sultan of Egypt awarded the Order of the Crescent in various sizes to the majority of officers present, and the Highland Society presented medals at their own expense to members of the 42nd Highlanders.

| a Gold (16) | £3500 | b Silver (2200) | £285 |
|---|---|---|---|

68

## Egypt 1801
## 69 Sultan's Medal (The Order of the Crescent)

This is often referred to as an Order, as it was issued in four different sizes or classes but it is in actual fact a service or campaign medal, awarded by Sultan Selim III to officers and NCOs who took part in the Egyptian campaign of 1801, when the French forces were expelled. The medal, which was suspended from a gold chain and hook, came in four sizes, namely 2.1in, 1.9in, 1.7in and 1.4in. All were given in gold to officers according to rank, but the smaller size was also awarded in silver to NCOs.

| | | | | | |
|---|---|---|---|---|---|
| a | Gold, 2.1in | £850 | d | Gold, 1.4in | £350 |
| b | Gold, 1.9in | £600 | e | Silver, 1.4in | £120 |
| c | Gold, 1.7in | £450 | | | |

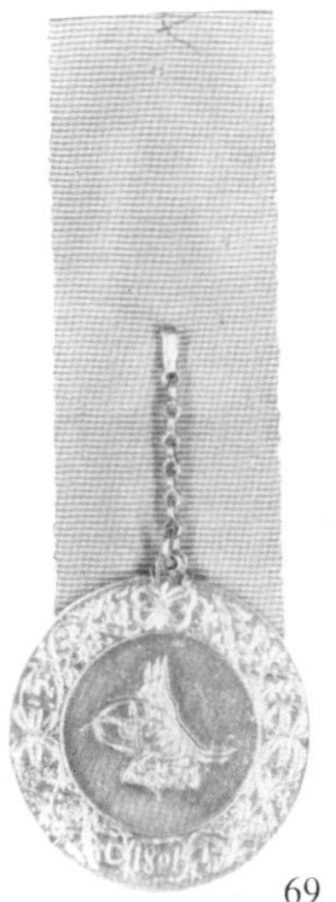
69

## 70 Egypt 1801 The Highland Society's Medal

This medal, which was awarded in both silver and bronze, was given by the Highland Society of London to the 42nd Highlanders (the Black Watch) for their action at Alexandria on 21st March 1801, where they captured a standard from Bonaparte's invincible legion. This seems to have been the first medal that can be traced as having been given to the next of kin of those killed in action.

| | | | | | |
|---|---|---|---|---|---|
| a | Silver | £150 | b | Bronze | £85 |

## 71 Trafalgar 1805 Mr Boulton's Medal

Mr Boulton, a manufacturer in Birmingham, at his own expense issued medals in various metals to the survivors of the Battle of Trafalgar. The medal is unusual in that around the edge there is an inscription, 'From M. Boulton to the Heroes of Trafalgar'. It was given in silver, bronze gilt, bronze and white metal, according to the rank of the recipient.

| | | | | | |
|---|---|---|---|---|---|
| a | Gold (1) | £7000 | d | Bronze | £200 |
| b | Silver | £485 | e | Pewter | £150 |
| c | Bronze gilt | £250 | | | |

71 72

## 72 Trafalgar 1805 Mr Davison's Medal

This was the second of two medals issued privately by Mr Davison, who was Nelson's prize agent, the first being for the Nile in 1798. This Trafalgar Medal was only issued in pewter and was awarded unnamed but is occasionally found crudely engraved on the reverse.

£325

73

## 73 The Medal for the Capture of Rodrigues, Isle of Bourbon and Isle of France 1809–10

Awarded by the East India Company to its forces from the Bombay and Bengal presidencies for the capture of the three islands of Rodrigues, Bourbon and France, which took place between July 1809 and the end of 1810. Fifty medals were awarded in gold and just over 2000 in silver; the medal is 1.9in in diameter and bears on the obverse a native holding a Union flag while standing before a gun. The reverse contains a wreath and a Persian inscription as well as one in English similar to the title above. Assistance was given by British troops and ships from the Royal Navy, who were not awarded any medals.

| | |
|---|---|
| a Gold (50) £3750 | b Silver (2200) £275 |

## 74 The Bagur and Palamos Medal 1810

Awarded by the Spanish Government to the crews of the *Ajax*, *Cambrian* and *Kent*. Eight medals were issued in gold to senior officers, while the remainder were awarded silver medals.

Some 600 seamen and marines landed to capture merchant ships which were tied up to the quays, although it transpired that the landing parties were driven through the town and eventually managed to return to their ships after suffering heavy casualties.

| | |
|---|---|
| a Gold (8) £3500 | b Silver (600) £200 |

## 75 The Java Medal 1811 (HEIC)

This medal was awarded by the HEIC for the capture of Java from Holland which had at that time become part of Napoleon's empire. Basically, the capture of Java was part of the British Government's policy of dominating the Far East at a time when

75 75

European forces were largely contained in Europe by the Royal Navy's blockade.

One hundred and thirty-three gold medals were issued and approximately 5750 silver (750 of these to Europeans), and these were awarded to officers and men of the Company's forces. The British forces were awarded medals much later on, in 1847—the Naval and Military General Service Medal with bar Java; the General and Field officers, as well as Naval captains, had previously been awarded gold medals. The obverse of the Company's medal depicts an attack on Fort Cornelis during the campaign and the reverse contains English and Persian inscriptions.

| a Gold (133) £3500 | b Silver (5750) £185 |
|---|---|

## 76 The Nepaul War Medal 1814–16 (HEIC)

76

This rather scarce medal, 2in in diameter, was awarded in silver, being issued to native troops only; approximately 350 were awarded. The medal was awarded for the campaign in Nepaul under Generals Marley, Gillespie (who was killed), and Ochterlony. The campaign was necessary so as to pacify the Rajah of Nepaul who had refused to ratify a treaty which had previously been signed by his ambassadors. The campaign was also undertaken so as to combat the frequent border raids made on the Company's territories by the Nepaulese. Since the date of the Treaty, Gurkha troops from Nepaul have been recruited into both the Indian and British Armies and their outstanding bravery and loyalty have become legendary. However, the use of the Gurkha troops outside the control of the British Crown is not permitted.

The obverse of the medal contains a scene of hills and stockades and the reverse a Persian inscription. The British troops and also the native troops who did not receive this medal were, in 1851, awarded the Army of India Medal with clasp Nepaul. The Nepaul Medal was struck by the Calcutta Mint and was normally worn suspended by a cord which passed through a loop attached to the award.

| Silver (350) | £265 |
|---|---|

## 77 The Ceylon Medal 1818

This particular medal was issued by the Ceylon Government for gallant conduct during the Kandian rebellion. Forty-five are supposed to have been issued, the regiments present being the 73rd Foot (2nd Battalion, the Black Watch) as well as the 1st and 2nd Ceylon Regiments.

| Silver (45) | £550 |
|---|---|

## 78 The Burma Medal 1824–26

78

This medal was authorized by the Honourable East India Company in 1826, being awarded to native officers and men in the Company's service, and was the first of the Company's 'modern' smaller size standard medals as we know them today. The war resulted from repeated acts of aggression by the Burmese on the borders adjacent to the East India Company's territory.

The obverse depicts the elephant of Ava kneeling before the British lion with palm trees and the Union flag, and an inscription is contained in the exergue. The reverse contains a scene of the storming of the pagoda at Rangoon. The medal was awarded to the Bengal and Madras Armies; native officers were presented with a gold medal, and the native troops a silver one. Approximately 740 gold medals were issued and 24,000 silver. The British troops involved were later, in 1851, issued with the Army of India Medal with bar Ava.

| | | | | | |
|---|---|---|---|---|---|
| a | Gold (750) | £750 | b | Silver (24,000) | £165 |

79

## 79 The Coorg Medal 1837

Awarded in gold and silver, only 44 of the gold and 300 of the silver being issued. The obverse depicts a Coorg warrior holding a knife in his raised right hand and musket in the left, with an inscription in Canarese which, translated, reads: 'A mark of favour given for loyalty to the Company's government in suppressing the rebellion in the months of April and May 1837'. The reverse contained war trophies and 'For Distinguished Conduct and Loyalty to the British Government of Coorg, April 1837'. The medal was issued solely to the Coorgs who remained loyal during the rebellion and was not awarded to the Company's regular or irregular forces.

Like many of the East India Company's medals, restrikes are found, many of which have die flaws.

| | | | | | |
|---|---|---|---|---|---|
| a | Gold (44) | £4000 | d | Silver (later striking) | £125 |
| b | Silver (300) | £300 | e | Bronze specimen | £80 |
| c | Gold (later striking) | £1250 | | | |

# Official Medals and Later Private Issues (nos. 80–167)

## 80 The Naval Gold Medal 1795–1815

This was introduced in 1795, two years after the commencement of the Napoleonic Wars and eighteen years before the equivalent Army Gold Crosses and Medals. The Naval Gold Medals were first introduced for award to admirals and captains of ships following Lord Howell's fleet victory over the French off Ushant on 1st June 1794, this generally being known as 'The Glorious 1st June'. The larger medals, which are 2in in diameter were awarded to admirals, and the smaller medals, 1.3in, to captains. Both medals were glazed on the obverse and reverse and were individually engraved on the reverse with details of the action and the recipient's name.

The whole series of medals is rare and consequently valuable, with only 22 of the larger and 117 of the smaller having been awarded. Following the victory in 1815, the medals were discontinued and successful officers after that date were awarded the Order of the Bath.

Officers who received the Naval Gold Medal also received, if they were living in 1847, the silver Naval General Service Medal for the action. Army officers who qualified for the military Gold Medals and Crosses did not receive the equivalent bars to their Military General Service Medal authorized in 1847.

80 a

a Small gold medal
1.3in dia. (117) £8500

b Large gold medal
2in dia. (22) £20,000

Only awarded for a few of the actions which were commemorated by the silver N.G.S. Medal issued in 1848, namely:

1st June 1794 (17:8)
*St Vincent* 1797 (15:6)
*Camperdown* 1797 (25:2)
Nile 1798 (14:1)
*Hermione* 1799 (1:–)
Trafalgar 1805 (27:3)
4th November 1805 (4:–)
St Domingo 1806 (8:2)
Curacao 1807 (4:–)
Capture of *Thetis* 1808 (1:–)
Capture of Badere Zaffer 1808 (1:–
Capture of *Furieuse* 1809 (1:–)
*Lissa* 1811 (4:–)
Banda Neira 1811 (1:–)
Capture of *Rivoli* 1812 (1:–)
Capture of *Chesapeake* 1813 (1:–)
Capture of *L'Etoile* 1814 (1:–)
*Endymion* with President 1815 (1:–)

*Numbers in brackets indicate small and large medals awarded thus: Trafalgar 27 small and 3 large medals*

## 81 Naval General Service Medal 1793–1840

The medal was not authorized until as late as 1847 and then it was only issued to those *still* surviving. Due to illiteracy, lack of communication and of publicity, many entitled to receive the award would not have claimed their medals and, as a result, the numbers issued for some of the approved actions were extremely few indeed. The medal was originally intended to cover the period of the Napoleonic Wars, namely 1793–1815, but the medal was then extended to cover the period up until 1840 so as to reward those that took part in the Battles of Algiers (1816), Navarino (1827) and Syria (1840). Some 24,000 medals were issued, but the majority, namely 21,000 had a single bar only; the maximum number of bars issued with one medal was seven, and only 1 was awarded; 5 medals had six bars and 14 medals were awarded with five bars.

The N.G.S. Medal is particularly interesting in that it was issued for actions against a multitude of nations, namely France, Holland, Spain, Denmark, Sweden, Turkey, Egypt, Algiers, USA and Russia, consequently, the medal is of intense interest to the collector. These actions, against all the major nations of the world at that time, were commemorated by the issue of 231 different bars. As with the majority of later medals, the medal was officially impressed, and the details can easily be checked against the superb medal roll produced by Captain K.J. Douglas-Morris, RN.

81

A selection of bars should give a general idea of price structure and for this purpose I have chosen bars covering general fleet actions, frigate actions and boat service engagements. Only single bar medals have been priced. The collector should bear in mind that *one cannot assess the value of a multiple bar medal by a simple addition of the values of the single bars.* In cases such as this, one's assessment should be based on the rarest bar and then add a small proportion only of the value of any further bars, etc.

Collectors must bear in mind that with this series in particular, one cannot assess a value simply based on the number of bars issued, otherwise Trafalgar would be of less value than, say, Algiers or Navarino and the Boat Service bar for 14th December 1814 would be less than that for all the other Boat Service bars listed! Various factors are taken into account such as the action itself, ie, whether it is a popular bar such as Trafalgar and which nation we engaged; those for services against the USA in the 1812–14 War are more in demand due to the interest of collectors in both countries. Another factor is the number of bars awarded to the ship which the recipient served aboard. Probably the most outstanding factor is the question of supply and demand and to assess this aspect a knowledge of the London market is essential. Because a medal fetches a particularly high price on one occasion it does not necessarily follow that a second would do likewise, as by that time some of the competition would have been removed.

| | *Fleet Actions* | |
|---|---|---|
| a | 1st June 1794 (583) | £700 |
| b | 14th March 1795 (114) | £850 |
| c | 23rd June 1795 (200) | £700 |
| d | St Vincent (364) | £800 |
| e | Camperdown (336) | £800 |
| f | Nile 1798 (351) | £800 |
| g | Egypt (511) | £600 |
| h | Copenhagen (545) | £800 |
| i | Gut of Gibraltar 1891 (153) | £550 |
| j | Trafalgar (1710) | £850 |
| k | 4th November 1805 (297) | £700 |
| l | Martinique (506) | £350 |
| m | Basque Roads (551) | £400 |
| n | Guadaloupe (484) | £350 |
| o | Java (695) | £300 |
| p | St Domingo (406) | £375 |
| q | St Sebastian (288) | £400 |
| r | Algiers (1362) | £250 |
| s | Navarino (1137) | £250 |
| t | Syria (7057) | £180 |

*Numbers in brackets indicate bars issued.*

| | *Frigate Actions* | |
|---|---|---|
| u | Mars 21st April 1798 (26) | £900 |
| v | Lion 15th July 1798 (21) | £1000 |
| w | Acre 30th May 1799 (42) | £750 |
| x | London 13th March 1806 (35) | £825 |
| y | Curacao 1st January 1807 (67) | £700 |
| z | Stately 22nd March 1808 (32) | £825 |
| | Lissa (132) | £450 |

| | *Boat Service Actions* | |
|---|---|---|
| aa | 16th July 1806 (53) | £650 |
| bb | 1st November 1809 (118) | £525 |
| cc | 28th June 1810 (26) | £900 |
| dd | 29th September 1812 (31) | £850 |
| ee | 2nd May 1813 (53) | £650 |
| ff | 8th April 1814 (24) | £1900 |
| gg | 14th December 1814 (214) | £1300 |

List of all bars and numbers awarded: *dates in italics are not included on the bar.*

Nymphe
18th June 1793 (4)
Crescent
20th Oct 1793 (12)
Zebra
17th March 1794 (2)
Carysfort
1st June 1794 (583)
Romney
17th June 1794 (2)
Blanche
4th Jan 1795 (5)
Lively
13th March 1795 (6)
14th March 1795 (114)
Astraea
10th April 1795 (2)
Hussar
17th May 1795 (1)
Thetis
17th May 1795 (2)
Mosquito
17th June 1795 (42)
23rd June 1795 (200)
Dido
24th June 1795 (1)
Lowestoffe
24th June 1795 (6)
Spider
25th August 1795 (1)
Port Spergui (4)
17th March 1796
Indefatigable
20th April 1796 (8)
Santa Margarita
8th June 1796 (3)
Unicorn
8th June 1796 (4)
Southampton
9th June 1796 (8)
Dryad
13th June 1796 (6)
Terpsichore
13th Oct 1796 (3)
Lapwing
3rd Dec 1796 (2)
Blanche
19th Dec 1796 (4)
Minerve
19th Dec 1796 (4)
Amazon
13th Jan 1797 (6)
Indefatigable
13th Jan 1797 (8)
St Vincent (364)
14th Feb 1797
Nymphe
8th March 1797 (5)
San Fiorenzo
8th March 1797 (8)
Camperdown (336)
(11th October, 1797)
Phoebe
21st Dec 1797 (5)
Mars
21st April 1798 (26)
Isle St Marcou (3)
6th May, 1798
Lion
15th July 1798 (23)
Nile (351)
(1st August 1798)
Espoir
7th Aug 1798 (1)
12th Oct 1798 (79)
Fisgard
20th Oct 1798 (9)
Sybille
28th Feb 1799 (12)
Acre
30th May 1799 (50)

Schiermonnikoog
12th Aug 1799 (9)
Arrow
13th Sept 1799 (2)
Surprise with
Hermione (7)
25th Oct 1799
Speedy
6th Nov 1799 (3)
Courier
22nd Nov 1799 (3)
Viper
26th Dec 1799 (2)
Fairy
5th Feb 1800 (4)
Harpy
5th Feb 1800 (4)
Loire
5th Feb 1800 (1)
Peterel
21st March 1800 (2)
Penelope
30th March 1800 (11)
Vinciego
30th March 1800 (2)
Capture of the
Désirée (24)
8th July 1800
Seine
20th Aug 1800 (7)
Phoebe
19th Feb 1801 (6)
Egypt (511)
8th March–22nd
Sept 1801
Copenhagen 1801 (545)
2nd April
Speedy
6th May 1801 (7)
Gut of Gibraltar
12th July 1801 (144)
Sylph
28th Sept 1801 (2)
Pasley
28th Oct 1801 (4)
Scorpion
31st March 1804 (4)
Centurion
18th Sept 1804 (12)
Acheron
3rd Feb 1805 (2)
Arrow
3rd Feb 1805 (8)
San Fiorenzo
14th Feb 1803 (13)
Phoenix
10th Aug 1803 (29)
Trafalgar (1710)
21st Oct 1805
4th Nov 1805 (297)
St Domingo (406)
6th Feb 1806
Amazon
13th March 1806 (30)
London
13th March 1806 (27)
Pique
26th March 1806 (8)
Sirius
17th April 1806 (20)

Blanche
19th July 1806 (22)
Anson
23rd Aug 1806 (11)
Arethusa
23rd Aug 1806 (17)
Curacao
1st Jan 1807 (67)
Pickle
3rd Jan 1807 (2)
Hydra
6th Aug 1807 (12)
Comus
15th Aug 1807 (9)
Louisa
28th Oct 1807 (1)
Carrier
4th Nov 1807 (1)
Sappho
2nd March 1808 (4)
San Fiorenzo
8th March 1808 (17)
Emerald
13th March 1808 (10)
Childers
14th March 1808 (4)
Nassau
22nd March 1808 (31)
Stately
22nd March 1808 (31)
Off Rota
4th April 1808 (19)
Grasshopper
24th April 1808 (7)
Rapid
24th April 1808 (1)
Redwing
7th May 1808 (7)
Virginie
19th May 1808 (21)
Redwing
31st May 1808 (7)
Seahorse with
Badere Zaffer (32)
(6th July 1808)
Comet
11th Aug 1808 (4)
Centaur
26th Aug 1808 (42)
Implacable
26th Aug 1808 (44)
Cruizer
1st Nov 1808 (4)
Amethyst wh. Thetis (31)
10th Nov 1808
Off the Pearl Rock
13th Dec 1808 (16)
Onyx
1st Jan 1809
Confiance
14th Jan 1809 (8)
Martinique (506)
2nd–10th Feb
1809
Horatio
10th Feb 1809 (13)
Superieure
10th Feb 1809 (1)
Amethyst
5th April 1809 (27)

Basque Roads 1809 (551)
12th April
Castor
17th June 1809 (7)
Pompee
17th June 1809 (47)
Recruit
17th June 1809 (13)
Cyane
25th and 27th
June 1809 (5)
L'Espoir
25th and 27th
June 1809 (5)
Bonne Citoyenne
with Furieuse (12)
6th July, 1809
Diana
11th Sept 1809 (8)
Anse la Barque
18th Dec 1809 (51)
Cherokee
10th Jan 1810 (4)
Scorpion
12th Jan 1810 (8)
Guadaloupe
Jan–Feb 1810 (484)
Firm
24th April 1810 (1)
Surly
24th April 1810 (1)
Sylvia
26th April 1810 (1)
Spartan
3rd May 1810 (30)
Royalist
May and June
1810 (3)
Amanthea
25th July 1810 (23)
Banda Neira (68)
9th Aug 1810
Otter
18th Sept 1810 (8)
Staunch
18th Sept 1810 (2)
Boadicea
18th Sept 1810 (15)
Briseis
14th Oct 1810 (2)
Lissa (124)
13th March
1811
Anholt
27th March 1811 (40)
Off Tamatave
20th May 1811 (87)
Hawke
18th Aug 1811 (6)
Java (695)
4th Aug–18th
Sept 1811
Locust
11th Nov 1811 (2)
Skylark
11th Nov 1811 (4)
Pelagosa
29th Nov 1811 (74)

Victorious wh.
Rivoli (67)
22nd Feb 1812
Weasel
22nd Feb 1812 (6)
Griffon
27th March 1812 (3)
Rosario
27th March 1812 (7)
Malaga
29th April 1812 (18)
Growler
22nd May 1812 (1)
Northumberland
22nd May 1812 (63)
Off Mardoe
6th July 1812 (47)
Sealark
21st July 1812 (4)
Royalist
29th Dec 1812 (4)
Weasel
22nd April 1813 (8)
Shannon wh.
Chesapeake (42)
1st June 1813
Pelican
14th Aug 1813 (4)
St Sebastian (288)
Aug–Sept 1813
Thunder
9th Oct 1813 (9)
Gluckstadt
5th Jan 1814 (45)
Cyane
16th Jan 1814 (7)
Venerable
16th Jan 1814 (42)
Eurotas
25th Feb 1814 (32)
Hebrus with
L'Etoile (40)
27th March
1814
Cherub
28th March 1814 (7)
Phoebe
28th March 1814 (36)
The Potomac
17th Aug 1814 (108)
Endymion wh.
President (58)
15th Jan 1815
Gaieta
24th July 1815 (89)
Algiers (1362)
27th Aug 1816
Navarino (1137)
20th Oct 1827
Syria (7057)
Nov 1840

BOAT SERVICE:

*Numbers in brackets indicate numbers issued*

15th March 1793 (1)
17th March 1794 (29)
29th May 1797 (3)
9th June 1799 (4)
20th Dec 1799 (3)
29th July 1800 (4)
29th Aug 1800 (25)
27th Oct 1800 (5)
21st July 1801 (7)
27th June 1803 (5)
4th Nov 1803 (1)
4th Feb 1804 (10)
4th June 1805 (10)
16th July 1806 (52)
2nd Jan 1807 (3)
21st Jan 1807 (8)
13th Feb 1808 (2)
10th July 1808 (8)
11th Aug 1808 (17)
28th Nov 1808 (2)
7th July 1809 (35)
14th July 1809 (7)
25th July 1809 (36)
27th July 1809 (10)
29th July 1809 (11)
28th Aug 1809 (15)
1st Nov 1809 (100)
13th Dec 1809 (9)
13th Feb 1810 (20)
1st May 1810 (15)
28th June 1810 (27)
27th Sept 1810 (36)
4th Nov 1810 (1)
23rd Nov 1810 (42)
24th Dec 1810 (6)
4th May 1811 (10)
30th July 1811 (4)
2nd Aug 1811 (9)
20th Sept 1811 (6)
4th Dec 1811 (19)
4th April 1812 (4)
1 and 18 Sept 1812 (21)
17th Sept 1812 (11)
29th Sept 1812 (25)
6th Jan 1813 (25)
21st March 1813 (3)
29th April 1813 (2)
April and May 1813 (56)
(29th April and
3rd May 1813)
2nd May 1813 (48)
8th April 1814 (24)
24th May 1814 (14)
3rd and 6th Sept
1814 (1)
14th Dec 1814 (205)

## 82 Army Gold Crosses and Medals 1806–14

Approved in 1813 by the Prince Regent on behalf of King George III, awarded to commemorate the victories of the Napoleonic Wars and also the American War of 1812–14. The gold medals were issued in two sizes, the larger was 2.1in in diameter and was restricted to general officers commanding, and the smaller, 1.3in in diameter, was awarded to officers who commanded regiments and battalions. As with the Naval Gold Medal, the Army Medals were glazed.

The name of the first action was engraved in the centre of the reverse, although that for Barrosa was die struck. In addition, a small special medal was struck in 1806 for Maida, which is part of the gold medals series.

A second or a third action was commemorated by a die-struck gold bar(s) which was attached to the riband. Officers who were engaged in more than three actions received a gold cross in lieu. The names of the four actions appeared on the arms of the cross, with additional bars added to the riband for five actions or more. In all, 163 crosses, and 85 large and 599 small medals were issued;

82 g

82 n

it therefore follows that the large gold medals are the rarest of this series. Following the successful conclusion of the peninsular War and prior to Waterloo, these gold awards were discontinued as by then the Order of the Bath had been enlarged to three classes with a military division and it then became the normal practice to award successful officers with one of the classes of the Bath.

Unlike Naval officers who received the Naval Gold Medal *and* also the silver Naval General Service Medal in 1848, Army officers did not receive the equivalent silver Military General Service Medal if they had been awarded the Gold Cross or Medal.

| | | | | |
|---|---|---|---|---|
| a | Maida 1806 | £15,000 | | |
| b | Small gold medal (field officers) 1.3in dia. | £2900 | (W. Indies) | £2300 |
| c | Small gold medal with 1 bar (field officers) | £3200 | | |
| d | Small gold medal with 2 bars (field officers) | £3500 | | |
| e | Small gold medal for Barrosa (die-struck reverse) | £4500 | | |
| f | Large gold medal (general officers) 2.1in dia. | £9000 | (W. Indies) | £6500 |
| g | Large gold medal (general officers) 2.1in with 1 bar | £9300 | | |
| h | large gold medal (general officers) 2.1in with 2 bars | £10,000 | | |
| i | Gold cross | £8000 | | |
| j | Gold cross with 1 bar | £8400 | | |
| k | Gold cross with 2 bars | £9000 | | |
| l | Gold cross with 3 bars | £9750 | | |
| m | Gold cross with 4 bars | £10,750 | | |
| n | Gold cross with 5 bars | £12,500 | | |

*(163 Crosses + 237 bars, 85 large + 43 bars and 599 small gold medals + 237 bars issued.)*
*All prices are for Peninsular actions unless otherwise stated.*

83 hh

## 83 The Military General Service Medal 1793–1814

As with the Naval General Service Medal of the same period, this medal was not authorized until 1847 and then issued only to the survivors living at that time. Some 25,650 applications were made for the medal, which was awarded with a variety of 29 different bars; the maximum number issued with any one medal was 15, and only two were issued; eleven medals were issued with 14 bars.

The principal reason for the issue of this medal was to reward Wellington's troops for their victories in Spain and Portugal, although bars were issued for places as far afield as Egypt in 1801, the East and West Indies, Italy and also for the 1812–14 war with America. Three bars were issued for the North American War, two of the place-names being in Canada, one in America—Fort Detroit, which is the only place-name to appear on a British military medal. Although the medal carries the date 1793, the first action commemorated by the medal was for Egypt 1801, this bar being issued after the other twenty-eight bars had been authorized. It has been said that the delay in the issue of the medal, some forty-six years lapsing between the first action and the issue, was due to the reluctance of the Duke of Wellington who was opposed to the issue of a standard medal to all ranks. However, when the medal was finally designed it incorporated in the reverse a likeness of the Duke, kneeling before the Queen (Victoria had come to the throne in the meantime) who is about to place a laurel wreath of victory on him.

83 ee
*(reverse)*

Unlike the Naval G.S. (No 81) this medal is far more frequently found with multiple bars although it was issued with a selection of only twenty-nine different bars. *Prices below are for single bar medals* and again, as with the Naval G.S., the addition of extra bars would normally only add a small proportion to the value. *In a number of cases, single-bar medals are more valuable than two- or three-bar medals.* The valuations for the multiple-bar medals are based on regiments where more than about a hundred bars were issued. However, one must bear in mind that prices can be expected to be higher where one or more of the bars is rare to a particular regiment, or of course if awarded to an officer.

| | | |
|---|---|---|
| a | Egypt | £250 |
| b | Maida | £280 |
| c | Roleia | £600 |
| d | Vimiera | £275 |
| e | Sahagun | £900 |
| f | Benevente | £1750 |
| g | Sahagun and Benevente | £375 |
| h | Corunna | £225 |
| i | Martinique (RN/RM £1200) | £240 |
| j | Talavera | £220 |
| k | Guadaloupe (RN/RM £1300) | £200 |
| l | Busaco | £250 |
| m | Barrosa | £250 |
| n | Fuentes D'Onor | £220 |
| o | Albuhera | £280 |
| p | Java (RN/RM £1100) | £240 |
| q | Ciudad Rodrigo | £350 |
| r | Badajoz | £240 |
| s | Salamanca | £260 |
| t | Fort Detroit | £1250 |

| | | |
|---|---|---|
| u | Chateaugay | £1200 |
| v | Chrystler's Farm | £950 |
| w | Vittoria | £190 |
| x | Pyrenees | £230 |
| y | St Sebastian | £190 |
| z | Nivelle | £240 |
| aa | Nive | £260 |
| bb | Orthes | £200 |
| cc | Toulouse | £180 |
| dd | 2 bar medal | £230 |
| ee | 3 bar medal | £260 |
| ff | 4 bar medal | £275 |
| gg | 5 bar medal | £320 |
| hh | 6 bar medal | £360 |
| ii | 7 bar medal | £410 |
| jj | 8 bar medal | £460 |
| kk | 9 bar medal | £500 |
| ll | 10 bar medal | £550 |
| mm | 11 bar medal | £775 |
| nn | 12 bar medal | £1075 |
| oo | 13 bar medal | £1750 |
| pp | 14 bar medal | £2500 |

*Single bars are often more scarce than a multiple-bar medal. Prices are based on medals to the most common units, however, medals to the King's German Legion are 25% lower in value.*

## 84 The Waterloo Medals 1815 (British and Allied)

84

This was the very first of the medals as we know them today, being awarded by the British Government to officers and other ranks alike. For the first time, the medals were officially named, thus making it possible for the recipient's service record and frequently, biographical details, to be checked, an aspect which always fascinates collectors. Although entitled 'The Waterloo Medal', the medal was issued to those that took part in one or more of the following battles; Ligny 16th June, Quatre Bras 16th June as well as Waterloo 18th June. In addition to receiving the medals, every soldier present was credited with two years' extra service.

Medals to those regiments that suffered casualties are more sought after and consequently a little more expensive than those to regiments which suffered lightly, or indeed than those who were in General Colville's Reserve Division and did not see any action. In addition to the British troops, medals were also issued to the King's German Legion. Details of casualties suffered by the various regiments can be found in *British Battles and Medals*, published by Spink & Son Ltd.

Unlike the Naval and Military General Service Medals issued in 1848 for the earlier Napoleonic campaigns, the Waterloo Medal was issued soon after the action, early in 1816; consequently, they were more frequently worn with the result that this medal is more difficult to find in really fine condition. Whether a medal is fitted with its original steel clip-ring, or with a fancy silver attachment at the recipient's expense, does not have any marked effect on the value.

The allies also issued medals of various designs to their own troops (84h, 1–5).

| | | |
|---|---|---|
| a | Heavy cavalry | £260 |
| b | Light cavalry | £240 |
| c | Foot guards | £275 |
| d | Foot regiments | £245 |
| e | RA etc | £220 |
| f | General Colville's reserve division 2/35th, 1/54th, 2/59th and 1/91st Foot | £210 |
| g | King's German Legion | £190 |
| h | Allies Waterloo medals | |
| | 1 Hanover | £120 |
| | 2 Brunswick | £160 |
| | 3 Dutch Star | £85 |
| | 4 Saxe-Gotha-Altenburg | £200 |
| | 5 Nassau | £110 |

## 85 The Army of India Medal 1799–1826

85t

This was the fourth and last medal to cover events connected directly or indirectly with the Napoleonic Wars. The Naval and Military General Services Medals, the Waterloo Medal and the Army of India Medal are considered by collectors as the 'classics' of a medal collection.

As with the two general service medals just referred to, the medal was not authorized until very much later on, namely 1851, and again was only issued to the survivors *living* at that time. It was awarded for the various battles and campaigns in India and Burma between 1803 and 1826; the medal carries on the obverse the effigy of Queen Victoria, who was not born when many of the actions were fought.

The medal is unusual in that the last bar awarded is placed nearest the medal, so that the correct sequence reads downwards. One medal was awarded with as many as 7 bars, and three received 6 bars. The medal was issued to those that took part in many very arduous campaigns and, if one takes into account the hardships and conditions of service against very determined enemies in an alien climate, one can more readily appreciate the award. The medal covered three separate wars, namely the second Maharata war 1803–04 (the first took place in 1778–84), the Nepal war of 1814–16 and the Pindaree, or third Maharata war, 1817–18. Major General Arthur Wellesley, later the Duke of Wellington, earned his 'spurs' in the second Maharata war and was often referred to later on as 'The Sepoy General'.

The medal, is more sought after when issued to the Sovereign's troops or to European officers and other ranks serving with the HEIC as opposed to those awarded to natives. The drawback to the medals awarded to natives is the difficulty of confirming the medal in the records, in addition to which, they were frequently issued engraved as opposed to the European medals which were invariably issued with impressed lettering. It follows that engraved medals are easier to fake.

---

*In spite of the fact that, of the 4500 medals awarded, nearly 4000 were issued with single bars, a number of the scarcer bars are more common when found in combination with others. Consequently, when considering the price of a particularly rare bar, I have chosen the more numerous issue, ie possibly a two- or three-bar combination; in cases such as these, the number of bars is shown in brackets, therefore, Assaye is the price of a medal with three different bars:*

| | | 1 *Imperial Regiments** | 2 *Natives* |
|---|---|---|---|
| a | Allighur (2 bar medal) | £2400 | £700 |
| b | Battle of Delhi (3 bar medal) | £2900 | £800 |
| c | Assaye (3 bar medal) | £2400 | £750 |
| d | Asseerghur (2 bar medal) | £2900 | £700 |
| e | laswarree (2 bar medal) | £2400 | £650 |
| f | Gawilghur (3 bar medal) | £2200 | £550 |
| g | Argaum (3 bar medal) | £2200 | £550 |
| h | Defence of Delhi | —— | £950 |
| i | Battle of Deig (2 bar medal) | £3400 | £700 |
| j | Capture of Deig (2 bar medal) | £2300 | £550 |
| k | Nepaul | £600 | £225 |
| l | Kirkee | —— | £675 |
| m | Poona | £2300 | £400 |
| n | Kirkee & Poona | £2400 | £600 |
| o | Seetabuldee | —— | £950 |
| p | Nagpoor | £850 | £375 |
| q | Seetabuldee & Nagpore | —— | £800 |
| r | maheidpoor | £1000 | £300 |
| s | Corygaum | —— | £850 |
| t | Ava (RN £550) | £425 | £175 |
| u | Bhurtpoor | £450 | £200 |
| v | Gilt *specimen* with the Duke of Wellington's bars. Gawilghur, Argaum, Assaye | £325 | |

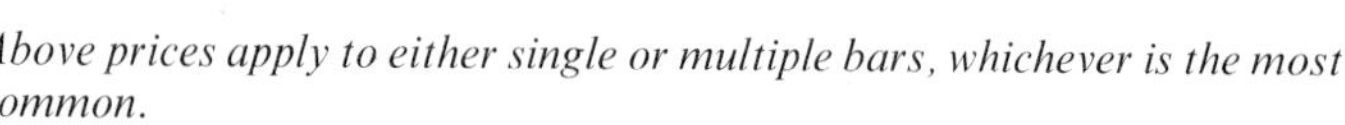

*Above prices apply to either single or multiple bars, whichever is the most common.*

* *These prices would apply to private Europeans in the HEIC's service.*

---

86

## 86 The Ghuznee Medal 1839

This was the first of many medals to be awarded for actions in connection with Afghanistan, an area which was to be a regular battleground for the armies in India during the next one hundred years, after which the Russians took over! This was the second campaign medal to be issued to British troops, the first being for

Waterloo 1815. The medal was awarded to both British and Indian troops who were present at the storming of and fighting around the fortress of Ghuznee between the 21st and 23rd July 1839. The purpose of the British presence in Afghanistan was to remove the anti-British King, Dost Mahomed, who had exiled his predecessor Shah Shojaah, and it appeared to the British that there was a distinct possibility that the regime of Dost Mahomed might associate itself with the Russians, in which case the presence of Russian troops would have endangered the whole of the Indian subcontinent.

The forces under the command of Dost Mahomed were defeated and Shah Shojaah was reinstated. To record his appreciation, the Shah instituted the Order of the Dooranie Empire (No 24) which was awarded in three different classes to British officers of field rank and above. The medal itself was issued at the expense of the Indian Government and was issued unnamed, although it is frequently found privately named in various styles.

a British troops £230
b Indian troops £150
c Unnamed £135

## 87 The St Jean d'Acre Medal 1840

87

Awarded by the Sultan of Turkey for the capture of Acre on the Syrian coast in 1840. This special medal was awarded in gold to naval captains, field officers and above, in silver to all other officers and warrant officers, and bronze to the remainder of the seamen, marines and soldiers. It was awarded to all who received the Naval General Service Medal with bar Syria (No 81), and is often found in a pair or group with British Service Medals.

a Gold £400
b Silver £60
c Bronze £35

## 88 The Candahar, Ghuznee and cabul Medals 1841–42

88 d

88 e

There were four varieties of this medal, all bearing on the obverse the diadem head of Queen Victoria with the legend '*Victoria Vindex*', while the reverses bore the name of the action or actions in cases where the recipient was involved in more than one of the battles. The different reverses read 'Candahar', 'Cabul', 'Ghuznee and Cabul', 'Candahar, Ghuznee and cabul'. The Cabul reverse was either spelt Cabul or Cabvl, the latter is very scarce.

The medals were issued to both the Queen's forces and those of the Company at the expense of the Honourable East India Company. These actions were at the commencement of almost one hundred years of activity against the mobile and warlike Afghans, which involved a succession of marches and counter-marches, defences and reliefs of fortresses, through hard winters and hot summers, when many regiments particularly distinguished themselves. The event which caused shock to the public was the virtual annihilation of the 44th Foot (the Essex Regiment)—only the doctor, Dr Bryden, managed to reach Jellalabad alive. The number of men killed in the Essex Regiment was 565, while 3 officers and 51 men were taken prisoner, 36 of them later being released by British troops.

| | 1 *Imperial Regiments* | 2 *Natives* | 3 *Unnamed* |
|---|---|---|---|
| a Candahar | £500 | £180 | £175 |
| b Cabul | £260 | £110 | £120 |
| c Cabvl ('Victoria Regina' legend) | £1100 | £800 | £250 |
| d Ghuznee/Cabul | £485 | £225 | £170 |
| e Candahar/Ghuznee/Cabul | £300 | £145 | £130 |

89 a

## 89 The Jellalabad Medal 1841–42

This medal was issued as one of the first Afghan War series, being presented by the Honourable East India Company. The medals were awarded to the surviving members of the garrison of Jellalabad which gallantly defended the fortress from the 12th November 1841 until 7th April 1842. There were two different types, one with a mural crown and one with a flying figure of Victory. Most of the next of kin of those killed received the flying Victory type.

| | 1 *Imperial Regiments* | 2 *Natives* | 3 *Unnamed* |
|---|---|---|---|
| *a* *1st type*: Obverse—mural crown 'Jellalabad' Reverse—'VII April 1842' | £300 | £150 | £100 |
| b *2nd type*: Obverse—bust of Victoria 'Victoria Vindex' Reverse—a winged figure of Victory 'Jellalabad VII April MDCCCXLII | £600 | £275 | £175 |

89 b

## 90 The Defence of Kelat-i-Ghilzie Medal 1842

This is the last of the medals issued by the Company to commemorate an action during the First Afghan War. This was the defence of the fortress of Kelat-i-Ghilzie, and the medal is particularly rare. None of the Queen's regiments were present, but forty European artillery and sixty sappers and miners of the Company's forces received the medal. In addition to these Europeans, the medal was awarded to 980 native troops, and few of these medals have survived.

a European recipients £3500 b Native recipients £585

90

## 91 The China War Medal 1842

The issue of such a medal, originally suggested by the Governor General of India, was for presentation to all ranks of the Honourable East India Company. However, it was subseqeuntly awarded by the British Government in 1843 and presented to those who had taken part in the capture of Chusan, the operation in Hangchow Bay and in the Canton River during 1841. The campaign ended with the capture of Nanking and, as a result of the war, the British took possession of Hong Kong. Medals were issued, the reverse depicted a lion with its forepaws on a dragon edges. The medal originally had a different design to that actually issued, then reverse depicted a lion with its forepaws on a dragon with 'Nanking 1842' in the exergue, but upon reflection, the British Government thought that the Chinese might consider the design to be offensive to them!

a Royal Navy £200 b Imperial Regts. £170 c Natives £110

91

92 c

## 92 The Scinde Campaign Medals 1843

The medal was issued with three different reverses which read either 'Meeanee', 'Hyderabad' or both 'Meeanee-Hyderabad', with all three versions having the date 1843 below the name of the battle(s). The medal was only issued to the 22nd Foot (the Cheshire Regiment) of the Queen's regiments, the remainder being awarded to the East India Company's forces, including four ships of the Indian Navy.

Following the end of the first Afghan War and the withdrawal of British and Indian troops, the Ameer of Scinde opened hostilities against the allied forces. The first task of the force, assembled under Major-General Sir Charles Napier, was the destruction of the fort of Emaum Ghur, situated in the desert. The action was described by the past master of military tactics, the Duke of Wellington, 'as one of the most curious military feats I have ever known to be performed.' General Napier set an example which has since been continuously followed, of naming in his official despatches NCOs and men who had specially distinguished themselves. These days such a 'mention' entitles one to wear a 'Mention in Despatches' emblem.

| | | 1 *European Members Indus Flotilla* | 2 *Natives Indus Flotilla* | 3 *Imperial Regiments* | 4 *Europeans in Indian Regiments* | 5 *Natives* | 6 *Unnamed* |
|---|---|---|---|---|---|---|---|
| a | Meeanee | £700 | £375 | £425 | £425 | £180 | £125 |
| b | Hyderabad | £600 | £325 | £425 | £275 | £150 | £125 |
| c | Meeanee-Hyderabad | —— | —— | £375 | £300 | £170 | £125 |

## 93 The Gwalior Campaign Stars 1843

These were issued in bronze, each having a silver centre impressed with the name of the action, which was either 'Maharajpoor' or Punniar' together with the date. The bronze stars were struck from guns captured from the enemy, thus preceding the policy of casting Victoria Crosses from captured Russian cannon. Both actions were fought on the same day, namely 29th December, and it was probably the shortest campaign for which medals were ever issued.

93 a

93 b

In spite of the very short duration of the actions, British losses were substantial.

At the time, peace manoeuvres were being carried out so as to overawe the population, but events soon changed to a war operation, and moved so quickly that four ladies who were spectators came under the fire of the Maharatta guns. Lord Ellenborough, the Governor General, presented these four ladies with gold and enamel stars bearing the effigy of Queen Victoria. The regiments that particularly distinguished themselves were Her Majesty's 16th Lancers, the 39th (the Dorsetshire Regiment) and the 40th Regiment (South Lancashire Regiment). The star issued for Punniar is scarcer than that issued for Maharajpoor.

| | | 1 *Imperial Regiments* | 2 *Natives* |
|---|---|---|---|
| a | Maharajpoor Star | £180 | £100 |
| b | Punniar Star | £220 | £110 |

## 94 The Sutlej Campaign Medal 1845–46

94 c

This was the first of the campaign medals which were issued with different bars and awarded to both officers and men alike (the medals for the earlier Napoleonic Wars which were issued with bars were not authorized until 1847). An unusual aspect of this medal is that the first action is mentioned in the reverse exergue of the medal, and those that were engaged in more than one action had a bar(s) placed above the medal suspender. The medal was issued to both the Queen's regiments and those of the East India Company. The 31st Regiment (East Surreys) and the 50th Foot (Royal Queen's West Kent Regiment) were the only British units that qualified for all four actions, consequently many of them received the medal with three bars which of course covered the four actions. The campaign was caused as a state of anarchy ruled in the Sutlej following the death of the ruler Runjeet Singh in 1839, which culminated in the Sikh army crossing the River Sutlej into the East Indoa Company's territory. The casualties were particularly severe, an aspect which was expected as the fighting qualities of the Sikh nation were renowned, in fact, the officers of the British regiments suffered some fifty per cent casualties and forty per cent to other ranks in a period of less than two months. To illustrate the fact that commanding officers of those days did not command from the rear, three major-generals and four brigadiers were killed, while one major-general and seven brigadiers were wounded.

| | | 1 *Imperial Regiments* | 2 *Natives* |
|---|---|---|---|
| a | Moodkee (18th December 1845) *Reverse* (no bar) | £185 | £105 |
| b | Moodkee *Reverse* with 1 bar | £220 | £135 |
| c | Moodkee *Reverse* with 2 bars | £280 | £175 |
| d | Moodkee *Reverse* with 3 bars | £425 | £240 |
| e | Ferozeshuhur (21st December 1845) *Reverse* no bar | £175 | £100 |
| f | Ferozeshuhur *Reverse* with 1 bar | £215 | £165 |
| g | Ferozeshuhur *Reverse* with 2 bars | £375 | £220 |
| h | Aliwal (28th January 1846) *Reverse* no bar | £165 | £100 |
| i | Aliwal *Reverse* with 1 bar | £200 | £170 |
| j | Sobraon (10th February 1846) *Reverse* no bar | £145 | £100 |

95 b

## 95 The Punjab Campaign Medal 1848–49

The actions for which this medal was awarded were really an extension to the Sikh war of 1845–46 (No. 94). The medal was issued with three different bars, the maximum to any one medal being two bars. As with the Sutlej Medal, this was awarded to both Europeans and to Indian troops, the medal being a little more common than that for the Sutlej. Medals to the South Wales Borderers (24th Foot) are eagerly sought after as about half the regiment became casualties at Chilianwala, while medals to the supporting Indus flotilla are also scarce. The reverse of the medal is thought to be one of the most attractive ever designed, showing General Sir Walter Gilbert on horseback receiving the surrender of the Sikh army, with a palm tree on a hill and inscription in the background. The fantastic diamond Koh-i-Noor, or Mountain of Light, was captured during the campaign and was later presented to Queen Victoria. The stone is now set in the crown for wear by a queen consort, which is permanently on display in the Jewel House in the Tower of London.

The 3 bars awarded were Mooltan, Chilianwala, Goojerat

| | | 1 *Imperial Regiments* | 2 *Natives* |
|---|---|---|---|
| a | No bar | £120 | £70 |
| b | 1 bar | £225 | £100 |
| c | 2 bars | £170 | £85 |
| d | Medals to casualties of the 24th Foot at Chilianwala (1 bar) | £275 | — |
| e | Medals without bars to the Indus flotilla (158) Europeans | £345 | £175 |
| f | Medals with 3 bars—specimen—gilt | £200 | — |

95 c
(*reverse*)

## 96 The South African Campaign Medal 1834–53

This medal was awarded for three different campaigns in southern Africa, namely 1834–35, 1846–47 and 1850–53. All received the same medal without bars and carrying the date 1853 on the reverse, consequently, it is impossible to tell which campaign or indeed campaigns the recipient had served in. The majority of the recipients were British troops although several hundred were issued to personnel who had served on five different ships. In addition, a few medals were awarded to local troops and officers.

Basically, the campaigns resulted from the aggressive warlike nature of the Kaffir tribes. These tribes made frequent raids on the settlers, making it necessary for military action to be undertaken. The Commanders-in-Chief were Major-General Sir Benjamin D'Uban, after whom Durban was named, and Sir Harry Smith, who was later Governor of Cape Province (the town of Ladysmith was named after his wife). The second campaign of 1846–47 was rather more hazardous, as by then many of the natives had acquired up-to-date firearms. The third and last campaign occured because the natives blockaded Sir Harry Smith in Fort Cox. Severe fighting subsequently took place with unexpected setbacks to the British troops.

An interesting sideline to this campaign was the sinking of the troopship *Birkenhead* off South Africa while on its way with reinforcements. The epic gallantry and outstanding discipline of the troops on board so impressed King William of Prussia that he had the full story read out at parades at every barracks in Germany.

96

| | | | |
|---|---|---|---|
| a Royal Navy | £225 | c Colonial Regiments | £185 |
| b Imperial Regiments | £200 | | |

Add £100 if proved to have been for the 1834–35 campaign and £75 for 1846–47

## 97 Sir Harry Smith's Medal for Gallantry 1851

This private medal is included and placed adjacent to the appropriate campaign medal, as it is of intense interest to collectors of medals awarded in connection with South Africa it is included in this section.

When the eighth Kaffir war commenced at the end of 1850, Sir Harry Smith was Governor and Commander-in-Chief at the Cape. During the early part of the war, Sir Harry was blockaded in Fort Cox in the vicinity of King Williamstown by the Gaikas tribe under Chief Sandilli. Eventually the C-in-C broke out of Fort Cox escorted by the Cape Mounted Riflemen and, being impressed by these men, he awarded a special silver medal.

| | |
|---|---|
| a Unnamed £450 | b Named £950 |

## 98 The India General Service Medal 1854–95

This was the first of several general service medals issued to cover minor campaigns in India and, unlike previous medals which were frequently awarded very many years or even decades after the actions, it was instituted as early as January 1854. The medal is found with numerous bars, and was never issued without at least one; twenty-three different bars were issued during the forty-year period. The majority were awarded for services on the Northern Frontiers of India, particularly the NW Frontier, others being issued for expeditions to Persia and Burma. As with most of the previous medals, this was issued in silver but, for the first time, the later medals from 1855 onwards were also issued in bronze, these

98 k

98 w (*reverse*)

being awarded to native support personnel such as transport drivers, servants and sweepers. The medal itself is very common, but some of the bars are rare, such as Kachin Hills 1892–93, Hunzar 1891 and Chin Hills 1892–93. Kachin Hills was awarded to the Yorkshire Regiment and Chin Hills to the Norfolk Regiment, these being the rarest of the whole series. The maximum number of bars to one medal appears to be seven.

Medals to European Privates in Indian regiments are assessed at 25% less value than to Imperial regiments

| | 1 *Royal & Indian Navies (Europeans)* | 2 *Indian Navy (Natives)* | 3 *Imperial Regiments* | 4 *Indian Regiments (Natives)* | 5 *Bronze* |
|---|---|---|---|---|---|
| a Pegu | £90 | £70 | £85 | £70 | —— |
| b Persia | £135 | £80 | £95 | £55 | —— |
| c NW Frontier | —— | —— | £85 | £40 | —— |
| d Umbeyla | —— | —— | £105 | £60 | —— |
| e Bhootun | —— | —— | £95 | £60 | —— |
| f Looshai | —— | —— | —— | £85 | —— |
| g Perak | £100 | £70 | £75 | £65 | —— |
| h Jowaki 1877–78 | —— | —— | £90 | £60 | —— |
| i Naga 1879–80 | —— | —— | —— | £145 | —— |
| j Burma 1885–87 | £75 | £65 | £55 | £35 | £45 |
| k Sikkim 1888 | —— | —— | £130 | £85 | £60 |
| l Hazara 1888 | —— | —— | £80 | £45 | £55 |
| m Burma 1887–89 | £85 | £65 | £60 | £30 | £50 |
| n Burma 1887–89 | £250 | —— | £250 | —— | —— |
| o Chin Lushai 1889–90 | £195 | £120 | £110 | £150 | £60 |
| p Lushai 1889–92 | —— | —— | £175 | £100 | £80 |
| q Samana 1891 | —— | —— | £90 | £50 | £40 |
| r Hazara 1891 | —— | —— | £100 | £45 | £40 |
| s NE Frontier 1891 | —— | —— | £100 | £65 | £45 |
| t Hunza 1891 | —— | —— | —— | £190 | £145 |
| u Burma 1889–91 | —— | —— | £60 | £45 | £35 |
| v Chin Hills 1892–93 | —— | —— | £325 | £120 | £100 |
| w Kachin Hills 1892–93 | —— | —— | £450 | £150 | £125 |
| x Waziristan 1894–95 | —— | —— | £100 | £40 | £45 |

## 99 The Baltic Medal 1854–55

99

This medal is associated with the Crimean War as the operations conducted in the Baltic against the Russian fleet were in general support of the Naval and Army operations in the Crimea. It was principally awarded to the Royal Navy and Royal Marines, but also awarded to approximately one hundred members of the sappers and miners who were with the fleet for demolition purposes. The British fleet consisted of about one hundred ships, including floats and mortar ships and was reinforced by a French fleet. Russian merchant ships were destroyed in the Gulfs of Bothnia and Rega, while the fortress of Bomarsund was attacked and later the fortress of Sveaborg.

The medals were issued unnamed but are, from time to time, found privately engraved, the exception being those issued to the Royal Sappers and Miners, which were officially impressed in the same style of lettering as the Crimea Medal.

| | | | |
|---|---|---|---|
| a Unnamed | £55 | d Officially impressed medals to the Sappers and Miners | £475 |
| b Engraved | £75 | | |
| c Impressed | £145 | | |

## 100 The Crimea Medals 1854–56

From Waterloo 1815 to the commencement of the First World War, a period of almost one hundred years, very many campaign medals were issued, but this was the only one awarded for services against a major power.

Queen Victoria was impressed by the deeds performed by her Army in the Crimea and she directed as early as 1854 that a medal be issued with the bars for Alma and Inkermann, which explains why the single date 1854 is to be found on the medal—the bars for Balaklava and Sebastopol were sanctioned in 1855. In addition to

100 g

a considerable number of medals awarded to the Navy and the Army, a few were also awarded to our French allies.

The war was due to Russian expansionist policies, principally directed at Turkey, then known as 'The Sick Man of Europe'. War was declared by both Britain and France at the same time, namely 28th May 1854 and the allies were later joined by the Italian kingdom of Sardinia.

The outstanding gallantry and extreme suffering of the troops during the campaign are now part and parcel of our history, and reflect the fact that the armed forces were ill-prepared to combat the hardships and climate that prevailed. The Army was led by many generals whose last active service was under Wellington during the Napoleonic Wars, and it is recorded that Lord Raglan, the C-in-C, often unthinkingly referred to the French as 'The Enemy'. Medals awarded to those that participated in the charges of the Light and Heavy Brigades are particularly sought after, as indeed are those that manned 'The Thin Red Line', namely the 93rd Highlanders.

The Turkish Government also awarded a service medal, which was issued to the French and British troops—approval was given by the British Government for this to be worn in uniform. There were three types and they seemed to have been issued indiscriminately; one had the wording 'Crimea 1855', supposedly for the British troops, 'La Crimée 1855' the French issue, or 'La Crimea 1854' the Italian/Sardinian issue.

The Italian/Sardinian Government also awarded a medal for valour to selected officers and men which was issued engraved.

5 bars were issued, but not more than 4 to a medal

| | | 1 *Unnamed* | 2 *Engraved or privately impressed* | 3 *Officially impressed to Army* | 4 *Officially impressed to RN/RM* |
|---|---|---|---|---|---|
| a | No bar | £35 | £45 | £55 | £75 |
| b | 1 bar Alma | £75 | £85 | £140 | —— |
| c | 1 bar Inkermann | £65 | £75 | £160 | £180 |
| d | 1 bar Azoff | £95 | £125 | —— | £190 |
| e | 1 bar Balaklava | £60 | £75 | £110 | —— |
| f | 1 bar Sebastopol | £45 | £50 | £80 | £100 |
| g | 2 bars (excluding Balaklava) | £65 | £75 | £145 | £165 |
| h | 3 bars (excluding Balaklava) | £90 | £110 | £170 | £220 |
| i | 4 bars | £110 | £150 | £240 | —— |

| | | 1 *Engraved, regimentally or privately impressed* | 2 *Officially impressed* |
|---|---|---|---|
| j | Heavy Brigade (4th & 5th Dragoon Gds, 1st, 2nd and 6th Dragoons) | £325 | £650 |
| k | Light Brigade (4th Light Dragoons, 8th and 11th Hussars, 13th Light Dragoons and 17th Lancers) | £750 | £2000 |
| l | Thin red line (93rd Foot) | £200 | £350 |

**Turkish Crimea Medals**

| | | |
|---|---|---|
| m | British, unnamed | £35 |
| n | British, named | £50 |
| o | French | £60 |
| p | Sardinian, unnamed | £25 |
| q | Sardinian, named | £30 |

**Sardinian Medal for Valour (named)** £175

## 101 The Indian Mutiny Medal 1857–58

The medal in question was awarded to those who had taken part in quelling the mutiny of the East India Company's troops. Basically, the mutiny resulted from unrest among some of the Indian princes and the population in general, trouble having been fermenting for many years. The final breaking point was caused as a result of the actions of the Indian Government who had annexed Oude, thus diminishing the power of the King. The Indian Medal was issued with five different bars, although the maximum number issued to one medal was four; fewer than 200 four-bar medals were awarded which were issued to the Bengal Artillery. The maximum number of bars that could be earned by the Queen's troops was three and these were awarded to those who qualified in the 9th Lancers. The most desirable medals are those issued for the *original* Defence of Lucknow, the Queen's regiment involved being the 32nd (Duke of Cornwall's) Light Infantry. Those awarded to the Naval Brigade are also sought after as the Brigade took part in no fewer than ten battles throughout the whole of India in its fifteen months of existence.

101 g

| | 1 *Navy* | 2 †*Imperial Troops* | 3 *Native Troops* |
|---|---|---|---|
| a No bar | £270 | £70 | £50 |
| b 1 bar Delhi | —— | £135 | £50 |
| c 1 bar Defence of Lucknow | —— | —— | —— |
| d 1 bar Relief of Lucknow | £250 | £140 | £85 |
| e 1 bar Lucknow | £250 | £140 | £85 |
| f 1 bar Central India | —— | £120 | £90 |
| g 2 bars* | £375 | £215 | £110 |
| h 3 bars* | —— | £350 | £185 |
| i 4 bars* | —— | —— | £250 |

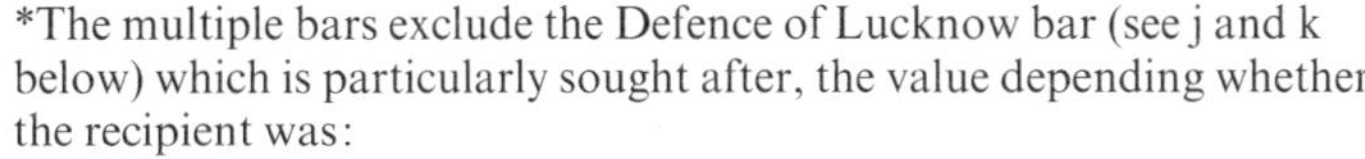
*The multiple bars exclude the Defence of Lucknow bar (see j and k below) which is particularly sought after, the value depending whether the recipient was:

| | †*Imperial Troops* |
|---|---|
| j an original defender | £675 |
| k *part of the 1st relief force | £345 |

†includes Europeans serving with Indian regiments and the HEIC

## 102 The China War Medal 1857–60

102 g

Like the Crimean War, this was another campaign in which the British and French forces co-ordinated, some 10,000 British and 7000 French servicemen participating.

The second China War (the first was fought between 1840–42) was caused due to various aggressive acts by the Chinese, among which was the seizure of the crew of the *Arrow*, sailing under British colours. During the first operations, the Navy and Marines only, under Admiral Sir Michael Seymour were involved. 11 British gunboats and about 50 ships defeated some 80 junks armed with 800 guns and manned by 6000 seamen. Having destroyed the fleet, all the British could do was to undertake the capture of Canton, which involved the Navy and the only British regiment there, the 59th (East Lancashire) regiment. This ended the first phase of the war, peace being signed on the 26th June 1858.

In the meantime, troops had been sent out from the UK, but they were diverted to quell the mutiny in India. The peace treaty, however, was not ratified, consequently hostilities again opened which involved considerable British land forces. The forts at the mouth of the River Peiho were captured, the occupation of Pekin took place and the summer palace at Pekin was destroyed by fire which took almost two days to burn out. Indiscriminate looting took place, many of the superb works of art are in western collections today.

None of the medals issued to the Navy were officially impressed

| | | 1 Unnamed | 2 Engraved Army | 3 Engraved Navy | 4 Officially impressed Army |
|---|---|---|---|---|---|
| a | No bar | £45 | £55 | £60 | £75 |
| b | 1 bar Fatshan 1857 | £80 | —— | £95 | —— |
| c | 1 bar Canton 1857 | £85 | £95 | £85 | £150 |
| d | 1 bar Taku Forts 1858 | £90 | —— | £95 | —— |
| e | 1 bar Taku Forts 1860 | £55 | £70 | £90 | £110 |
| f | 1 bar Pekin 1860 | £60 | £70 | £80 | £130 |
| g | 2 bars | £70 | £85 | £90 | £130 |
| h | 3 bars | £90 | £110 | £110 | £180 |
| i | 4 bars | £135 | —— | £175 | —— |
| j | 5 bars (specimen) | £250 | —— | —— | —— |

*The above prices do not include the bar China 1842 which is difficult to verify*

103 c
(*reverse*)

## 103 The Canada General Service Medal 1866–70

This medal was not approved until as late as January 1899, some thirty years after the event. The medal was issued by the Canadian Government to both British forces and the Canadian local forces for participation in the rebellions of 1866 and 1870. Almost 17,600 medals were awarded, the majority, over 15,000, being given to Canadians, with just over 2000 going to the British Army and Navy.

The campaign took place following the end of the American Civil War, when large numbers of soldiers were available for recruitment by the Fenians. Their aim was to cause embarrassment to Britain so as to endeavour to establish a united Irish Republic, and they therefore organized an invasion of Canada from the United States.

Less than a dozen medals were issued with three bars, while 1400 were awarded with two bars, and a few medals were issued to the Royal Navy, which command higher prices than those awarded to the Army.

| | | 1 Canadian Units | 2 Imperial Regiments | 3 Royal Navy |
|---|---|---|---|---|
| a | Fenian Raid 1866 | £125 | £150 | £220 |
| b | Fenian Raid 1870 | £150 | £170 | —— |
| c | Red River 1870 | £800 | £850 | —— |
| d | 2 bars Fenian Raid 1866 and 1870 | £250 | £300 | —— |
| e | 3 bars | £2500 | —— | —— |

*Multiple bars should be carefully verified*

103 b

## 104 The Abyssinian War Medal 1867–68

This campaign resulted from King Theodore of Abyssinia imprisoning the British Consul and other British subjects as well as a number of foreigners. After negotiations, the prisoners were released, but in a short time they were rearrested together with the negotiators! As a result of the campaign, the capital of those days, Magala, was captured and razed to the ground, the King committed suicide and peace terms were concluded.

The medal was sanctioned in 1869 and was probably the most expensive of the campaign medals ever to be produced as the recipient's name and unit, etc were embossed in the centre of the reverse which necessitated an expensive manufacturing operation. Those awarded to the Indian troops had their names impressed or engraved in the more normal way. 12,000 were awarded to the British Army and 2000 to the Royal Navy, who were under the general command of Lieutenant-General Sir Robert Napier (later Lord Napier of Magdala). The Navy landed a small brigade of one hundred to man the rockets and casualties amounted to only two killed and twenty-seven wounded, this was probably one of the most successful of the Victorian campaigns. As a result of the lack of casualties and blood and thunder generally, the medal does not attract the attention of collectors to the same extent as medals for, say, the Crimea or the Indian Mutiny. Later on, in 1896, the Italians attempted a similar expedition, but their forces suffered almost total annihilation at Adowa.

| | | | | | |
|---|---|---|---|---|---|
| a | British regiments | £160 | c | Indian troops | £95 |
| b | Royal Navy | £170 | d | RN Rocket Brigade | £325 |

104

## 105 The New Zealand Medal 1845–47 and 1860–66

The reverse of this medal differs from all others in the series in that the recipient's dates of service are die struck in the centre. In addition, medals were issued without dates signifying service in either the first or second war. The medal was authorized in 1869, consequently some of the recipients had to wait twenty-four years before receiving their medals (the medal was only issued to those that survived to 1869). Many of the dates are rare, particularly those issued to naval ships for the first of the wars.

It was not until about 1839 that the first British settlers arrived in New Zealand and a treaty was agreed with the Maoris regarding the purchase of lands. Not surprisingly, it was not very long before the increase in the number of settlers placed considerable strain on relations with the Maori tribes, with the result that fighting broke

105

105 w

out. The second war came about due to the same reasons as the first, and it was in this war that the Maori tribes proved themselves to be quite remarkable antagonists, their bravery causing considerable British casualties. Peace was declared in 1866 and, from that time onwards, relationships between the proud Maoris and the settlers improved, with the result that complete integration has taken place, both nations being equally respected in all walks of life.

It was during the latter part of the wars that the New Zealand Cross (No 24) was introduced (without the approval of Queen Victoria) as local volunteer forces did not qualify for the Victoria Cross.

---

The period of service is contained on the reverse in raised digits. Those issued undated could be awarded for either the first or the second of the Maori uprisings. Instances where *very* rare odd dates were awarded have been ignored as it is almost impossible to arrive at a fair price structure.

| | *First war* | 1 *Navy* | 2 *Army* | 3 *Local volunteers* |
|---|---|---|---|---|
| a | Undated | —— | £135 | —— |
| b | 1845–46 | £280 | —— | —— |
| c | 1845–47 | £475 | —— | —— |
| d | 1846–47 | £400 | —— | —— |
| e | 1846 | £800 | —— | —— |
| f | 1847 | £650 | —— | —— |
| g | 1848 | —— | £2500 | —— |
| | *Second war* | | | |
| h | Undated | —— | £85 | £110 |
| i | 1860 | £1000 | £950 | —— |
| j | 1860–61 | £175 | £500 | —— |
| k | 1860–63 | —— | £1600 | —— |
| l | 1860–64 | —— | £225 | —— |
| m | 1860–65 | —— | £200 | —— |
| n | 1860–66 | —— | £200 | —— |
| o | 1861 | —— | £1850 | —— |
| p | 1861–63 | —— | —— | —— |
| q | 1861–64 | —— | £250 | —— |
| r | 1861–65 | —— | £2500 | —— |
| s | 1861–66 | —— | £175 | £225 |
| t | 1862–66 | —— | —— | —— |
| u | 1863 | —— | £450 | £150 |
| v | 1863–64 | £165 | £220 | —— |
| w | 1863–65 | £350 | £200 | —— |
| x | 1863–66 | —— | £175 | —— |
| y | 1864 | £875 | £225 | £275 |
| z | 1864–65 | —— | £200 | —— |
| aa | 1864–66 | —— | £150 | —— |
| bb | 1865 | £850 | £900 | —— |
| cc | 1865–66 | —— | £155 | —— |
| dd | 1866 | —— | £170 | —— |

---

106 b

## 106 The Ashantee War Medal 1873–74

The Port of Lemina in the Ashanti was Dutch territory but this was then transferred to the British. The Dutch had made a practice of giving King Coffee an annual payment for the use of the port but this ceased when the British took over and, as a result, hostilities broke out. During the early part of the campaign, the fighting was, naturally, on the coast and this was largely undertaken by a small force of Marines and the Royal Navy. The advance on, and the capture of Kumasi the capital was undertaken in a period lasting one month only, but during this short period four Victoria Crosses were awarded. A small Naval detachment under Captain Glover, known as 'Glover's Force', was ordered to attack Kumasi in the rear, which caused King Coffee to sue for peace, whereupon he had to pay an indemnity demanded by the British C-in-C General Wolsey. The rate of sickness during the campaign was extremely high, some ninety-eight per cent of the Naval forces engaged on land reported sick during the period. The medal was issued with bar 'Coomassie', this being awarded to those who took part in the attack on the capital. Silver medals were also awarded to natives, a few of which were in bronze, which are quite scarce. These natives were recruited locally by the Navy and their medals are sometimes found officially inscribed with the very amusing names given to them by the crews of the ships, such as Pea Soup, Bottle of Beer, Prince of Wales and Tom Twoglass, etc.

| | | 1 *Royal Navy* | 2 *Army* | 3 *Natives* | 4 *Bronze* |
|---|---|---|---|---|---|
| a | No bar | £120 | £130 | £100 | —— |
| b | Bar Coomassie | £300 | £175 | £140 | £500 |

## 107 The South African Medal 1877–79

This medal was of the same design as that for the earlier wars fought between 1835–53, except that the reverse date '1853' in the exergue is replaced by a Zulu shield and four crossed assegais. While the earlier medal was issued without a bar, this was issued either without a bar or with one of the bars listed below.

The campaign came about largely due to tribal conflicts, principally the attack by the Galeka and Gaikas tribes on the Fingoes, the latter being under British protection. The disturbances spread which made it necessary for fairly large contingents from the Army, Navy and local units to become involved. Possibly the most notable and disastrous event from the British point of view was the Zulu nation's attack on Lord Chelmsford's columns near the border at Isandhlwana, where more than 1300 British troops, including the 24th Foot (South of Wales Borderers) and native followers were annihilated. After that, the Zulus moved on some ten miles to the post at Rorke's Drift, and here the small garrison of 139 men who were guarding the sick and wounded were attacked by 3000 Zulus. During the defence, no fewer than eleven Victoria Crosses were awarded. The campaign eventually ended successfully, after the defeat of the Zulus at Ulundi.

107 g

| | | 1 *Royal Navy* | 2 *Army* | 3 *Colonial* |
|---|---|---|---|---|
| a | Without bar | £100 | £95 | £100 |
| b | 1877 | —— | —— | £450 |
| c | 1877–78 | £350 | £220 | £225 |
| d | 1877–8–9 | £400 | £210 | £225 |
| e | 1878 | —— | £220 | £250 |
| f | 1878–79 | £325 | £240 | £300 |
| g | 1879 | £150 | £120 | £130 |
| h | Rorke's Drift participant | —— | £4000 | —— |
| i | Isandhlwana | —— | £2500 | —— |

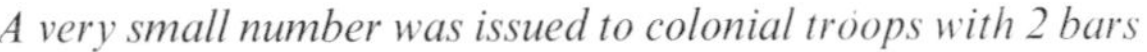

*A very small number was issued to colonial troops with 2 bars*

## 108 The Afghan War Medal 1878–80

This medal commemorates the second Afghan War, the first wars having been fought in the early 1840s for which medals were issued

109

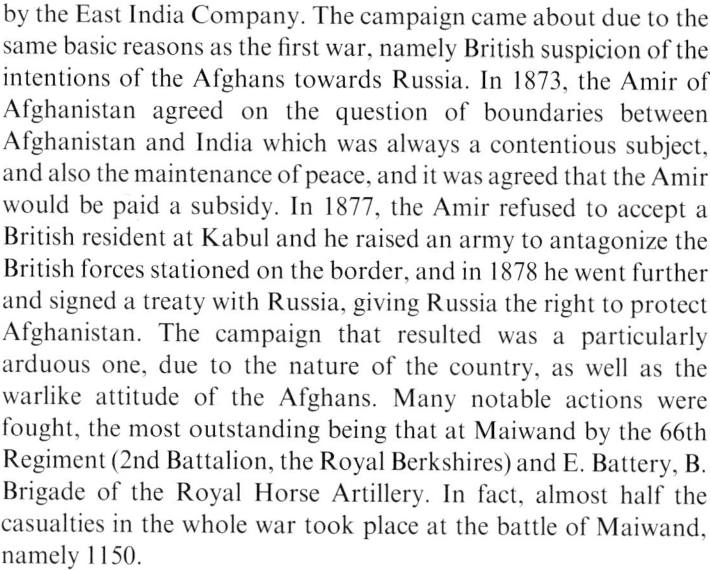
by the East India Company. The campaign came about due to the same basic reasons as the first war, namely British suspicion of the intentions of the Afghans towards Russia. In 1873, the Amir of Afghanistan agreed on the question of boundaries between Afghanistan and India which was always a contentious subject, and also the maintenance of peace, and it was agreed that the Amir would be paid a subsidy. In 1877, the Amir refused to accept a British resident at Kabul and he raised an army to antagonize the British forces stationed on the border, and in 1878 he went further and signed a treaty with Russia, giving Russia the right to protect Afghanistan. The campaign that resulted was a particularly arduous one, due to the nature of the country, as well as the warlike attitude of the Afghans. Many notable actions were fought, the most outstanding being that at Maiwand by the 66th Regiment (2nd Battalion, the Royal Berkshires) and E. Battery, B. Brigade of the Royal Horse Artillery. In fact, almost half the casualties in the whole war took place at the battle of Maiwand, namely 1150.

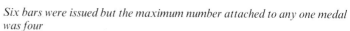

*Six bars were issued but the maximum number attached to any one medal was four*

| | | 1 *Imperial Regiments* | 2 *Natives* |
|---|---|---|---|
| a | No bar bronze | —— | £200 |
| b | No bar silver | £45 | £35 |
| c | 1 bar Ali Musjid | £65 | £45 |
| d | 1 bar Peiwar Kotal | £75 | £50 |
| e | 1 bar Charasia | £75 | £50 |
| f | 1 bar Kabul | £65 | £45 |
| g | 1 bar Ahmed Khel | £85 | £55 |
| h | 1 bar Kandahar | £60 | £40 |
| i | 2 bars | £100 | £55 |
| j | 3 bars | £140 | £75 |
| k | 4 bars | £240 | £140 |
| l | Killed at Maiwand<br>1 66th Foot (Berkshires)<br>2 E.Bty B.Bde RA | £375 | —— |

110 c

## 109 The Kabul to Kandahar Star 1880

The design of this star, which was manufactured in bronze from captured guns, shows a total departure from the normal circular medal. The stars were struck by a private company in Birmingham, H. Jenkins & Sons, and were awarded together with the silver medal with bar Kandahar. These were presented to those who had taken part in the famous march by General Roberts of just over 300 miles from the capital of Kabul to relieve the garrison at Kandahar; both British and Indian troops were involved. The relief of the garrison at Kandahar and the action that took place soon afterwards in the vicinity effectively ended the war, although the border area could never be described as being particularly peaceful.

| | | |
|---|---|---|
| a | Impressed naming on reverse to British troops | £80 |
| b | Engraved naming on reverse to Indian troops | £40 |

110 c (*reverse*)

## 110 The Cape of Good Hope General Service Medal 1880–97

Awarded in silver by the Cape Government in 1900 for services in suppressing small uprisings in the Transkei, Basutoland and Bechuanaland. Basically, the disturbances were caused due to resentment by the natives to the peace terms, which followed the defeat of Chief Moirosi, that dictated that all arms were to be handed in. Another resentment was the fact that serious outbreaks of cattle desease occurred in Bechuanaland, which led to the slaughter of large numbers of the natives' cattle.

The medals were awarded to local, regular and volunteer regiments and were issued with up to three bars, but only twenty-three were awarded with the maximum number.

*Numbers in brackets indicate numbers awarded*

| | | | | | |
|---|---|---|---|---|---|
| a | Transkei (1070) | £375 | d | 2 bars | £475 |
| b | Basutoland (2150) | £225 | e | 3 bars (23) | £900 |
| c | Bechuanaland (2580) | £200 | | | |

## 111 The Egypt Medal 1882–89

The Suez Canal was opened in 1869 which made the strategic position of Egypt even more important from the British point of view. Due to the general financial chaos that prevailed in Egypt, the Egyptian Army was not paid and, as a result, mutinied. Events then took a turn for the worse, and the Arabs attacked the Europeans. Early in 1882, a combined British and French squadron of ships arrived off Alexandria and sent ultimatums ashore which were ignored. As a result, the forts at Alexandria were attacked and destroyed and the canal seized by a combined British force consisting of Naval and Army units. The French, although they arrived with the British off Alexandria, took no part in the conflict and withdrew.

A second phase opened in 1884, much further south in the Sudan, where a new leader who was proclaimed 'The Mahdi' raised a force which annihilated the British and Egyptian troops; this caused the need for another combined British and Army operation. General Gordon was in command with a besieged garrison at Khartoum the capital of Sudan, but unfortunately the

111 *l*

111 j

British forces failed to relieve him and he and his garrison were overwhelmed. Further events caused other actions up until as late as August 1889, but it was not until the battle of Toski had taken place that the general area was made more peaceful. The operation caused considerable problems of transportation on the River Nile, and to overcome these problems boatmen were recruited from as far away as Canada, who were employed for their particular skill and experience in shooting rapids which were of particular value in the taking of supplies up and down the Nile. Thomas Cook the travel agent was also employed by the Government to convey personnel and stores up and down the Nile. Could this have been one of the first of their package tours?!

The maximum number of bars that were issued with one medal was 7, but only one was awarded, six were awarded with 6 bars, while those with 5 bars are far from common. The blue and white riband represents the Blue and White Niles with the major river, the Blue Nile, being represented by three blue stripes and the lesser Nile, the White, by two white stripes.

| | | 1 **Royal Navy* | 2 *Army* |
|---|---|---|---|
| a | No bar | £40 | £40 |
| b | Alexandria | £50 | —— |
| c | Tel-el-Kebir | £55 | £55 |
| d | El-Teb | £145 | £95 |
| e | Tamaai | £110 | £85 |
| f | El-Teb-Tamaai | £100 | £90 |
| g | Suakin 1884 | £65 | £65 |
| h | The Nile 1884–85 | £55 | £55 |
| i | Abu Klea (not awarded singly, with 'The Nile 1884–85') | £300 | £140 |
| j | Kirbekan (not awarded singly, with 'The Nile 1884–85') | £300 | £130 |
| k | Suakin 1885 | £65 | £60 |
| l | Tofrek (generally not awarded singly, with Suakin 1885) | £200 | £140 |
| m | Gemaizah | £120 | £100 |
| n | Toski | £180 | £100 |
| o | 2 bars | £85 | £75 |
| p | 3 bars | £140 | £120 |
| q | 4 bars | £250 | £220 |
| r | 5 bars | —— | £425 |

* including Royal Marines where medal is named to one of HM ships

*Multiple bars based on the most common combination, odd detached menhave been ignored*

| | | |
|---|---|---|
| s | Medals to Canadian boatmen | £650 |
| t | Medals to new South Wales Arty. (Suakin 1885) | £500 |
| u | Medals to natives (in Arabic), prices as above but less 40% | |

## 112 The Khedive of Egypt's Star 1882–91

112 b

Issued by the Khedive of Egypt having been authorized by the Sultan of the Ottoman Empire. It was presented in appreciation of the services rendered by the British Army and Navy, etc and was awarded to all those who received the British Medal (See No 111). The medal was privately struck by H. Jenkins of Birmingham and awarded with three different dates. There was also an undated type with or without a bar for Tokar, which was issued in 1891.

| | | | | | |
|---|---|---|---|---|---|
| a | Undated | £25 | d | 1884 | £35 |
| b | Undated with Tokar clasp | £60 | e | 1884–86 | £30 |
| c | 1882 | £20 | | | |

*All were issued unnamed*

## 113 The North West Canada Medal 1885

113 b

It is rather strange that the earlier campaign medal for services in Canada against the Fenians 1866–70 (No. 103) was not authorized until 1899, and yet this one for 1885 was authorized immediately by the Canadian Government. British troops were not engaged except for sixteen officers who were on the staff in Canada at the time. Some 5600 medals were awarded, these being issued unnamed, although some are found privately named. The medal was awarded with or without one bar, namely Saskatchewan. Just occasionally, an unofficial bar is found reading Batouche. Medals to the Steamer *Northcote* are eagerly sought after as only thirty-four were awarded. The North-west Mounted Police were involved, but strangely enough they did not receive a medal, having been awarded a grant of 320 acres of land or 80 dollars script in lieu.

Basically, the campaign came about due to the reaction of the local population to new settlers. In this case, the construction of the Canadian Pacific Railway was taking place which opened the prairies to white settlers, thus presenting a threat to the Métis, or half-breeds, who were squatters on the land likely to be granted to the new settlers. In spite of representations to the Government by the half-breeds, no agreement was reached, and Riel, who had been involved in the rising of 1866–70, led an uprising. This was his last rebellion as he was hung upon his capture in 1885.

| | | 1 *Named* | 2 *Unnamed* |
|---|---|---|---|
| a | No bar | £175 | £100 |
| b | Bar Saskatchewan | £345 | £165 |
| c | To the steamer *Northcote* | £600 | —— |

## 114 The Royal Niger Company's Medal 1886–97

Nigeria was administered by the Royal Niger Company in a similar manner to the East India Company's rule of India prior to the Indian Mutiny. In 1899, the Company's charter was revoked and the administration of the territory which is present-day Nigeria was then taken over by the Imperial Government.

The medals were struck on behalf of the Company, being designed and produced by the London company Spink & Son Ltd.

The medal is quite scarce as fewer than 100 silver medals were awarded to officers and NCOs for participation in numerous small expeditions against the tribes in Nigeria. Approximately 250 medals were issued in bronze to natives. They were issued in both silver (named) and bronze (numbered). Later marked specimens from the original dies appear on the market—*details appear in* British Battles & Medals.

| | | | | | |
|---|---|---|---|---|---|
| a | Silver with bar Nigeria 1886–97 (*named*) | £375 | c | Bronze with bar Nigeria (*numbered*) | £225 |
| b | Silver with bar Nigeria 1886–97. Unnamed specimen. | £85 | d | Bronze with bar Nigeria Unnumbered specimen. | £65 |

## 115 The East and West African Medal 1887–1900

This medal is another in the 'general' series being issued for numerous small campaigns and expeditions during the period 1887–1900. Twenty-two different bars were awarded, but the action for M'Wele, 1895–96, for some curious reason was engraved on the rim of the medal instead of a bar being awarded. The medal was issued in silver but is occasionally found in bronze, the latter being awarded to native servants, etc. Medals were not awarded to British regiments as a whole, although officers and NCOs seconded to native regiments, for example, as instructors, had their parent regiment impressed on the rim of the medal. Many of the bars were awarded to the personnel of Royal Naval ships which were very active off the coast and on the rivers. Twenty-three bars were issued, those for Liwondi 1893, Juba River 1893, Dawkita 1897 and Lake Nyasa are the rarest. The campaign on Lake Nyasa was only accomplished by the assistance of the ships *Adventure* and *Pioneer*, which had to be hauled in sections over two hundred miles of virgin country and then assembled on the shore of Lake Nyasa.

114 c

115 b

| | | 1 *Royal Navy* | 2 *Natives* |
|---|---|---|---|
| a | 1887–88 | £300 | £180 |
| b | Witu 1890 | £140 | £225 |
| c | 1891–92 | £190 | £200 |
| d | 1892 | £225 | £120 |
| e | Witu August 1893 | £190 | £180 |
| f | Liwondi | £2000 | —— |
| g | Lake Nyasa | £1800 | —— |
| h | Juba River 1893 | £1900 | —— |
| i | 1893–94 (*Colonial Steamer*) | £200 | £200 |
| j | Gambia 1894 | £150 | £200 |
| k | Benin River 1894 | £240 | £200 |
| l | Brass River 1895 | £200 | —— |
| m | Mwele 1895–96 (*on the edge of the medal*) | £180 | £100 |
| n | Bronze Mwele 1895–96 (*on the edge of the medal*) | —— | £350 |
| o | 1896–98 | —— | £300 |
| p | Niger 1897 | —— | £425 |
| q | Benin 1897 | £125 | —— |
| r | Dawkita 1897 | —— | £2500 |
| s | 1897–98 | —— | £120 |
| t | 1898 | £900 | £200 |
| u | Sierra Leone 1898–99 | £185 | £120 |
| v | 1899 | £900 | £275 |
| w | 1900 | —— | £350 |

*In the case of a multiple-bar medal, consider the basic value of the rarer bar and add 25% of the value of the more common bars. If to an officer consult the extra values shown on page 10. Odd detached or seconded men have not been included.*

## 116 The British South Africa Company's Medal 1890–97

This was another of the semi-private issues, being awarded by the Company for services in the campaigns in Mashonaland, Matabeleland and Rhodesia and unlike some private issues, Queen Victoria sanctioned that they be allowed to be worn in uniform.

116

116 (*reverse*)

116 b, with 1 bar

The reverse of the medal is particularly striking as it depicts a charging lion with a spear sticking in its chest, in the background is a mimosa bush and in the foreground a native shield and spears. Four recipients were entitled to the medal with 4 bars, but only one was known to be issued; twelve medals were awarded with 3 bars. The medal was issued to both Imperial troops and to local units. That with the reverse reading 'Rhodesia 1896' was the commonest issue.

The name of the first campaign is contained on the reverse of this medal (with the exception of Mashonaland 1890), with a bar(s) to denote subsequent engagements. The Mashonaland 1890 campaign was not recognized until 1927 when a similar medal was issued but without place, name or date on the reverse, the medal being issued with a bar for the campaign.

| | | 1 *British Regiments* | 2 *Colonial Units* |
|---|---|---|---|
| a | Mashonaland 1890 (bar) | —— | £1300 |
| b | Matabeleland 1893 (reverse) | £275 | £225 |
| c | Rhodesia 1896 (reverse) | £175 | £140 |
| d | Mashonaland 1897 (reverse) | £300 | £240 |
| e | Rhodesia (reverse) with 1 bar | £225 | £220 |

## 117 The Central Africa Medal 1891–98

Awarded for participation in a number of small expeditions in Central Africa in the general area of what is now Uganda. British troops were not entitled to this medal, although a few officers and NCOs who were attached as, for example, instructors, were awarded the medal which was in silver, although just a few were issued to native servants in bronze. This is one of several medals issued for service in and around Africa during the latter half of the nineteenth century, which was a period when the different spheres of European interest were taking shape. The riband is divided into three equal stripes of black, white and terracotta, representing the Africans, Europeans and Indians.

| | | |
|---|---|---|
| a | Without bar with ring suspender | £185 |
| b | With bar Central Africa 1894–98 with ring suspender | £220 |
| c | With bar Central Africa and straight bar suspender | £400 |
| d | With bar Central Africa and straight bar suspender in bronze | £450 |
| | *Prices based on medals to natives* | |

117 a

117 c

118

## 118 Hunza Naga Badge 1891

This is in the form of a plaque, being produced in London upon the instruction of the Maharaja of Jummoo (Jammu) and Kashmir for award to his own troops who also received the I.G.S. 1854 medal (No. 98) with bar Hunza 1891.

£100

## 119 The Hong Kong Plague Medal 1894

119

This medal was awarded by the community of Hong Kong to three hundred men of the King's Shropshire Light Infantry and fifty members of the Navy and Royal Engineers as well as to a few members of the local police. The medal was not authorized to be worn on uniform, but it is more than likely, due to the very lax regulations of the period, that the medals were worn from time to time. In addition to the silver medals, fifty were awarded in gold to officers and possibly a few to nursing sisters.

The medal was awarded for service in 1894 during the severe epidemic of bubonic plague. The epidemic broke out near Canton and then in May, gained a foothold in Hong Kong; over 2500 people died during a three-month period.

The obverse design is very symbolic, showing a Chinaman lying on a trestle table leaning against a man who is fending off a winged figure of death with his left hand, while a woman is bending over the sick man. On a scroll in the exergue is the date 1894, and to the left is a Chinese inscription.

| | 1 *Royal Navy* | 2 *Royal Engineers* | 3 *King's Shropshire Light Infantry* |
|---|---|---|---|
| a Gold | £900 | £850 | £850 |
| b Silver | £475 | £450 | £425 |

## 120 The Indian General Service Medal 1895–1902

This medal was introduced to replace the I.G.S. medal 1854–95 which had been awarded for the last forty years, having a total of twenty-three different bars, consequently, there was a need for an entirely new design and new issue.

The medal was issued with two different obverses, the first bore the crowned head of Queen Victoria, and the second the head and shoulders of Edward VII in field marshal's uniform.

As with the previous medal, this was issued for services mostly on the North-West Frontier over a six-year period. Six different bars were awarded, the rarest being that for the Defence of Chitral followed by Malakand. Unlike the earlier medal, all issues were awarded in silver *and* bronze; they were issued to British and Indian regiments but not to the Royal Navy.

120 d
(*reverse*)

120 a

120 g

| | | 1 *British Regiments (Silver)* | 2 *Indian Regiments (Silver)* | 3 *Bronze* |
|---|---|---|---|---|
| a | Defence of Chitral | —— | £650 | £300 |
| b | Relief of Chitral | £70 | £50 | £40 |
| c | Punjab Frontier 1897–98 | £60 | £40 | £40 |
| d | Malakand 1897 | £160 | £85 | £70 |
| e | Samana 1897* | £180 | £70 | £60 |
| f | Tirah 1897–98* | £115 | £60 | £50 |
| g | Waziristan 1901–02 (Edward VII obverse) | —— | £40 | £45 |
| | *Not awarded as single bars, prices are for 2 bar combination. | | | |
| | Multiple bars (excluding Defence of Chitral and Malakand) | | | |
| h | 2 bars | £80 | £55 | £60 |
| i | 3 bars | £120 | £65 | £70 |
| j | 4 bars | —— | £85 | £95 |
| k | 5 bars | —— | £125 | £125 |

121

## 121 The Jummoo and Kashmir Medal 1895

Awarded by the Maharajah of Jummoo (Jammu) and Kashmir to the native levies who took part in the Defence of Chitral 1895, an event covered by a bar to the Indian General Service 1895 Medal (No. 120). The bronze medal, which was produced in London, is unusual in that it is kidney-shaped.

£90

## 122 The Queen's Sudan Medal 1896–97

Issued in 1899 in both silver and bronze but the latter are quite scarce. Unlike many other issues, the medal was issued without bars. The medal was awarded to all the forces engaged in the reconquest of the Sudan between 1896–98, the principal actions being Firket, Hafir, Abu Hamed, Sudan 1897, the Atbara and

122

122 (*reverse*)

Khartoum. The latter was connected with the Battle of Omdurman, where the British 21st Lancers made their gallant charge against a very large and determined enemy force. Some five hundred casualties were incurred by the British before Khartoum.

The medal was awarded to commemorate the reconquest of the Sudan, which followed Britain's departure some years before. The half-yellow and half-black colours on the riband represent the desert and the Sudanese nation while the narrow red stripe in the centre is symbolic of the British Army and Navy.

| | | | | | |
|---|---|---|---|---|---|
| a | Silver | £65 | c | Bronze (unnamed) | £120 |
| b | Silver, to those of the 21st Lancers who took part in the cavalry charge at Omdurman | £250 | d | Bronze (named) | £200 |

## 123 The Khedive's Sudan Medal 1896–1908

The medal was authorized by a special Egyptian Army order on 12th February 1897 to commemorate the reconquest of the Dongola province. The medal was issued with as many as fifteen different bars, but is rare with more than two bars, 'The Atbara' and 'Khartoum', to British troops. Approval was given for the medal to be worn in uniform. The medal was issued in both silver and bronze but is very scarce in the latter metal.

It was awarded to both British and Egyptian Armies as well as to the Royal Navy who manned the river steamers on the Nile. The yellow of the riband represents the deserts, while the central blue stripe the Blue Nile which, with the specially built railway, was the main supply artery.

123 r

| | | | | | |
|---|---|---|---|---|---|
| a | No bar (silver) | £45 | i | Gederef | £100 |
| b | No bar (bronze) | £110 | j | Gedid | £120 |
| c | Firket | £80 | k | Sudan 1899 | £90 |
| d | Hafir | £90 | l | Bahr-el-Ghaza 1900–02 | £130 |
| e | Abu Hamed | £100 | m | Jerok | £140 |
| f | Sudan 1897 | £120 | n | Nyam-Nyam | £130 |
| g | The Atbara (*as a single bar to British troops*) | £145 | o | Talodi | £130 |
| h | Khartoum (British Regt) | £60 | p | Katfia | £140 |
| | Multiple bars, unnamed to natives | | q | Nyima | £120 |
| r | 2 bars | £80 | v | 6 bars | £120 |
| s | 3 bars | £85 | w | 7 bars | £140 |
| t | 4 bars | £100 | x | 8 bars | £160 |
| u | 5 bars | £110 | | | |

*Prices are based on named medals to Indians and Arabs with the exception of The Atbara and Khartoum; the latter two were mostly awarded to British regiments.*

## 124 Gordon's Star for Khartoum

During the time General Gordon was beseiged in Khartoum, he had cast a star for distribution to his officers and troops with the idea of raising morale. Recipients had to buy the award and the funds went to relieve the poor. The design was based on the Turkish Order of Medjidie and the stars were crudely cast in sand. They are found not only in pewter but also in gold-plated pewter and it is also thought that Gordon had a few cast in silver.

| | | | | | |
|---|---|---|---|---|---|
| a | Pewter | £60 | b | Pewter gilt | £100 |

## 125 The Ashanti Star 1896

This unusual-looking bronze medal is in the form of a four-pointed star, together with the cross of St Andrew. The medal was struck in bronze with a dull gun-metal finish. The recipients' names were not officially engraved on the medals, as was the case with most issues, the reverses simply reading 'From the Queen'. However, the Colonel of the West Yorkshire Regiment, which was the only regiment present in force, had the medals of his 2nd Battalion named at his own expense. It is said that the star was designed by Princess Henry of Battenburg whose husband died of fever in the campaign. The star was awarded to some 2000 troops who took part in the Ashanti expedition under Major-General F.C. Scott against King Prempeh, who had been indulging in cannibalism and human sacrifices. The campaign culminated in the capture of the capital Kumasi, which is now part of Ghana.

125

| | | | | | |
|---|---|---|---|---|---|
| a | Unnamed as issued | £70 | b | Regimentally named (West Yorks) | £95 |

## 126 The British North Borneo Company's Medals 1897–1937

This is another in the series of medals issued by a trading company such as those awarded by the Honourable East India Company and the Royal Niger Company.

The medals were awarded for various expeditions in the areas which are now Sarawak, Brunei and Sabah, the first and last states forming part of the present-day Federation of Malay States. The medals were issued in silver and bronze (except Rundum) to both British and native officials and servants, and a small number of Sikh troops. British subjects, however, were not permitted to wear the medal except in Borneo. The medals were produced by Spink & Son Ltd of London.

| | *Silver* | | *Bronze* | |
|---|---|---|---|---|
| | 1 *Original* | 2 *Specimen* | 3 *Original* | 4 *Specimen* |
| a Punitive Expedition | £300 | £90 | £170 | £55 |
| b Punitive Expeditions | £300 | £90 | £170 | £55 |
| c Tambunan | £350 | £90 | £200 | £55 |
| d Rundum | £375 | £90 | (*Not issued in bronze*) | |
| e General Service Medal, issued without a bar, in silver only | £200 | £90 | — | — |

*Specimens are struck from heavy gauge blanks or with 'S' of Spink or 'S' of Son on the reverse deleted. The G.S. specimen has the tip of the wreath in the exergue stamped out.*

## 127 The East and Central Africa Medal 1897–99

Mainly awarded in silver, but a few were issued in bronze to camp followers. The medal was awarded for operations in Uganda and Southern Sudan and was issued to local units such as the Uganda Rifles and various regiments from India. British recipients were mostly officers in command of these regiments.

| | | | |
|---|---|---|---|
| a | Bar Lubwa's (as a 2 bar medal only) | £320 |
| b | 1 bar Uganda 1897–98 | £225 |
| c | 1 bar 1898 (silver) | £245 |
| d | 1 bar 1898 (bronze) | £400 |
| e | 1 bar Uganda 1899 | £245 |

*Prices are for medals named to natives*

127 c

## 128 The Queen's South Africa Medals 1899–1902

Relations between the British Government and the Boers had never been exactly cordial, however, the latter's hostility was not confined just to the British as they had rebelled against the Dutch East India Company. Prior to the British conquest of the Cape of Good Hope and from the very early stages of settlement there had been constant friction between the Boers and the natives. War finally came about due to an ultimatum handed into the British agent in Pretoria.

The Boers from the very outset assumed the offensive, while the British, owing to their numerical inferiority, were compelled to act strictly on the defensive until the arrival of reinforcements from England. Eventually, the number of troops involved were very considerable and it came about that the Queen's South Africa Medal was issued in very large numbers. It was issued with a variety of twenty-six bars, the maximum number of bars issued with any one medal was nine to the Army and eight to the Navy. Various units were involved for the first time, such as the balloon and photographic sections, cyclist units, field force canteens as well as units from Canada, Australia and New Zealand. In addition, volunteer battalions from all over the British Isles served in South Africa.

There were two varieties of medal, the second having a reverse

128 s

128 d

128 ee

reading 'Mediterranean', which were awarded to the 3rd Battalions of certain British regiments who had the rather onerous task of guarding the numerous Boer prisoners on the island of St Helena. The medals were issued in silver but a few in bronze were issued without bars which were awarded to local natives, Indian troops and members of West Indian regiments. Due to the large number of medals issued, the variety of bars and the very wide range of units involved, the medal is particularly suitable for collecting, especially by the beginner.

It should be noted that some bars are rarer when issued singly as opposed to multiple-bar combinations, whilst in a few cases single bars were not issued. Single-bar prices are placed first with the most common multiple-bar combinations following in brackets £x). Medals with reverse dates in relief (*not* ghost dates) are rare.

| | | 1 *Royal Navy* | 2 *Imperial Regiments* | 3 *South African Units* | 4 *Australian & New Zealand* | 5 *Canadian Regiments* |
|---|---|---|---|---|---|---|
| a | Without bar (bronze) | — — | — — | £40 — | — — | — — |
| b | Without bar (silver) | £45 — | £30 — | £70 — | £85 — | £125 — |
| c | Cape Colony | £50 (£45) | £30 (£30) | £30 (£30) | £40 (£40) | £100 (£100) |
| d | Rhodesia | — — | — — | £125 (£85) | £90 (£60) | £300 (£250) |
| e | Relief of Mafeking | — — | — — | £150 (£60) | £180 (£140) | £350 (£300) |
| f | Defence of Kimberley | — — | £150 (£100) | £100 (£60) | — — | — — |
| g | Talana | — — | £75 (£110) | £150 (£70) | — — | — — |
| h | Elandslaagte | — — | £125 (£75) | — — | — — | — — |
| i | Defence of Ladysmith | £100 — | £50 (£60) | £120 (£60) | — — | — — |
| j | Belmont | £160 (£60) | £40 (£35) | — — | £225 (£175) | — — |
| k | Modder River | — (£65) | £100 (£35) | — — | £225 (£175) | — — |
| l | Tugela Heights | — — | — (£35) | — — | — — | — — |
| m | Natal | £50 (£200) | £40 (£55) | £150 (£55) | — — | £200 (£180) |
| n | Relief of Kimberley | — (£120) | £125 (£40) | £160 (£40) | £125 (£90) | — — |
| o | Paardeberg | — (£45) | £125 (£40) | £170 (£50) | £90 (£70) | £140 (£120) |
| p | Orange Free State | — (£120) | £45 (£30) | £120 (£30) | £90 (£45) | £120 (£100) |
| q | Relief of Ladysmith | £260 (£70) | £50 (£40) | £120 (£50) | — — | — — |
| r | Driefontein | — (£65) | £140 (£35) | — — | £55 (£40) | £185 (£160) |
| s | Wepener | — — | £125 (£240) | £150 (£140) | — — | — — |
| t | Defence of Mafeking | — — | — — | £850 (£850) | — — | — — |
| u | Transvaal | — (£60) | £25 (£30) | £30 (£35) | £65 (£45) | £200 (£170) |
| v | Johannesburg | — (£70) | £100 (£40) | £140 (£45) | £65 (£45) | £140 (£120) |
| w | Laing's Nek | — (£80) | £85 (£50) | — — | — — | — — |
| x | Diamond Hill | — (£80) | £85 (£40) | £140 (£50) | £70 (£50) | £200 (£170) |
| y | Wittebergen | — — | £40 (£30) | £160 (£80) | £75 (£50) | — — |
| z | Belfast | — (£70) | £90 (£50) | — (£45) | £75 (£50) | £140 (£120) |
| aa | S. Africa 1901 | — (£60) | £40 (£35) | £110 (£30) | £150 (£50) | £180 (£140) |
| bb | S. Africa 1902 | — (£120) | £50 (£35) | £110 (£30) | — (£60) | £140 (£110) |
| cc | 2 bars | £45 | £30 | £35 | £70 | £100 |
| dd | 3 bars | £65 | £35 | £40 | £90 | £110 |
| ee | 4 bars | £75 | £35 | £40 | £120 | £130 |
| ff | 5 bars | £85 | £40 | £45 | £140 | £185 |
| gg | 6 bars | £100 | £55 | £85 | £200 | £250 |
| hh | 7 bars | £150 | £100 | £145 | £350 | — |
| ii | 8 bars | £250 | £200 | £375 | — | — |
| jj | Relief dates on reverse (Canadian) | | £1450 | | | |
| kk | Nurses | | £70 | | | |
| ll | War correspondents | | £350 | | | |
| mm | MEDITERRANEAN MEDAL | | £110 | | | |

– indicates bar not issued, for this purpose 'odd' detached men have been ignored.

The 2nd price shown in brackets indicates the value of the most common multiple-bar combination which, in most cases, is of less value than a single-bar medal.

*Prices for medals to S. African, Australian, New Zealand and Canadian units are based on the current UK price structure. For details of medals to the RN, refer to a forthcoming specialist publication by W. H. Fevyer—which will be available from Spink & Son Ltd.*

129

## 129 The King's South Africa Medal 1901–02

This medal was never issued without the Queen's Medal, neither was it issued without a bar, except in the case of nurses (plus a few 'odd' men), who received almost 600 medals. The medal commemorated service in South Africa during the latter part of the Boer War in 1901–02, although in actual fact the official surrender of the Boers came about in 1900. The medal commemorates the very many minor actions, which were mostly guerilla, in 1901 and 1902. Very few King's Medals were awarded to the Royal Navy as the Naval brigades had returned to their ships in 1901.

| | | |
|---|---|---|
| a | No bar (nurses) | £60 |
| b | 2 bars 1901 & 1902 (nurses) | £300 |
| c | 2 bars 1901 & 1902 (RN) | £400 |
| d | 2 bars 1901 & 1902 (Army) | £20 |

## 130 The Yorkshire Imperial Yeomanry Medal 1900–02

Many different medals were issued by towns and boroughs, etc, to local troops who served in the Boer War, which are the subject of a book entitled *Boer War Tribute Medals* by M. G. Hibbard. The medals issued to the Yorkshire Imperial Yeomanry are included in this catalogue as more were issued than any other and they often appear on dealers' lists.

The medal was awarded to the 3rd and 66th Imperial Yeomanry Battalions with different reverse dates. All were produced by Spink & Son Ltd in London.

| | | |
|---|---|---|
| a | 3rd Imperial Yeo. S. Africa 1900–01 | £35 |
| b | 3rd Imperial Yeo. S. Africa 1901–02 | £45 |
| c | 66th Imperial Yeo. S. Africa 1900–01 | £45 |

## 131 The Medal for the Defence of Ookiep 1902

This medal, in silver to officers and in bronze to other ranks, was awarded for the Defence of Ookiep in Namaqualand, the siege lasting from 4th April–4th May 1902. Ookiep was the centre of the Cape Copper Mining Company's operations. When Smuts, a

131

131 (*reverse*)

commando leader (later Field Marshal, Prime Minister of South Africa and a member of the Imperial War Cabinet), invaded the district, the garrison in the area retired on Ookiep, the defence of which was commanded by Major Dean, the Company's manager. The garrison consisted of 660 half-castes, 206 European miners and 44 men of the 9th Warwickshire militia, as well as 12 men of the Cape garrison artillery. The total strength was just over 900 officers and men.

| a Silver £1250 | b Bronze £600 |
|---|---|

## 132 The Anglo Boer War Medal 1899–1902

Authorized by the Government of the Union of South Africa in 1920, some 14,000 medals were distributed to all ranks of the Boer forces who had distinguished themselves in the Boer War of 1899–1902. The curious feature of this medal is that, if it were worn by somebody from the Transvaal, he wore the medal so that the arms of the Transvaal were on the obverse and if a Free-Stater, then he had the arms of the Orange Free State as the obverse.

£55

132 132

## 133 The Defence of Kimberley Star 1899–1900

133

This is one of a fairly extensive series of private medals awarded by, for example, individuals and towns in both South Africa and the United Kingdom. This was awarded by, or in the name of, the Mayor of Kimberley to those involved in the defence of the town against the Boers. Although a local and private issue, a number of medals awarded as mementoes to British troops.

See *Boer War Tribute Medals* by M. G. Hibbard for a comprehensive study of the series.

£50

134 a    134 b

## 134 The Transport Medal 1899–1902

This medal was introduced for award solely to the Mercantile Marine. The unusual feature of the medal is that it was restricted solely to the master, the 1st, 2nd and 3rd officers, 1st, 2nd and 3rd engineers, pursers and surgeons only. The medal was issued in silver to these officers with a bar(s) reading either South Africa and/or China, which covered the Boer and the Boxer Wars of 1900. 1270 medals were awarded with the bar South Africa 1899–1902 and 323 with the bar China 1900, while 188 only had both bars. In both cases, the medals with bars were awarded for transporting troops, etc, by sea.

| | | 1 *Masters* | 2 *Other Officers* |
|---|---|---|---|
| a | 1 bar S. Africa 1899–1902 | £240 | £220 |
| b | 1 bar China 1900 | £360 | £300 |
| c | 2 bars | £450 | £375 |

## 134a The St John Ambulance Brigade Medal for South Africa

A bronze medal was issued by the Order of St John to the members of the St John Ambulance Brigade who served in South Africa during the Boer War or who took an active part in mobilization, training or despatch of comforts. A total of 1871 were issued, all were engraved on the rim with the name and unit of the recipient and often the medal is found associated with the Queen's and King's South Africa Medals. Fourteen members of the brigade who travelled to China from South Africa aboard the hospital ship USS *Maine* were awarded the China Medal.

£65

## 135 The Ashanti War Medal 1900

135 b

This was the first campaign medal authorized during the reign of Edward VII and was issued in silver to combatants and in bronze to native transport personnel, etc. Some 3500 medals were issued in silver, while a little less than 1000 were in bronze. In addition to the 3500 silver issued to the natives, approximately 170 were issued to British officers and NCOs.

The Ashanti uprising was sparked off by the Governor's attempt to take possession of the 'Golden Stool', which was the symbol of authority in the Ashanti. As a result, the Governor was beseiged in the capital Kumassi (which, incidentally, is spelt differently on this occasion). It became necessary to evacuate the capital and it was not until a little later on that two large columns recaptured the city. British troops did not participate as a whole as they were heavily involved in events in South Africa and China.

| | 1 *Silver* | 2 *Bronze* |
|---|---|---|
| a Without bar | £110 | £140 |
| b Bar Kumassi | £240 | £185 |

*Based on awards to natives*

## 136 The China War Medal 1900

136 g

This is the third and last of the medals awarded for services against China, unless we consider the Naval General Service Medal with bar for Yangtze 1949. Three bars were issued, but the most that could be issued with one medal was only two. The majority of the medals were issued in silver, native servants and followers received their medals in bronze.

The war broke out due to the persecution of European missionaries and traders by the various Chinese secret societies, commonly known as Boxers. As the Chinese Government was not able or willing to curtail their activities, the Royal Navy commenced hostilities under the command of Admiral Sir Edward Seymour. An international force was quickly raised comprising units from America, France, Japan, Russia and Germany, under the overall command of the German Field Marshal, Count Von Waldersee. Until the relief force arrived, Peking had to be defended by the small garrisons maintained by most of the legations. The British legation guard comprised, among others, some eighty members of the Royal Marines and naturally, their medals with bars 'Defence of Legations', are particularly sought after.

| | 1 *Royal Navy* | 2 *Army* | 3 *Native Regiments* |
|---|---|---|---|
| a No bar (bronze) | — | — | £60 |
| b No bar (silver) | £70 | £65 | £45 |
| c 1 bar Taku Forts (silver) | £265 | £110 | £90 |
| d 1 bar Defence of Legations (silver) | £1950 | — | — |
| e 1 bar Relief of Pekin (silver) | £130 | £185 | £75 |
| f 1 bar Relief of Pekin (bronze) | — | — | £100 |
| g 2 bars (excluding Defence of Legations) | £325 | £240 | £175 |

## 137 The Africa General Service Medal 1902–56

This medal was introduced to replace the East and West Africa Medal 1887–1900, to which twenty-two bars had already been issued. This 1902 medal was in existence for fifty-four years, which was the longest survival rating of all British Service medals.

The medal was issued with the obverse effigies of King Edward VII, George V and Queen Elizabeth II, no bars being awarded during the reign of King George VI (1936–52). Thirty-four bars were awarded during the short reign of Edward VII, ten with George V and one only with Queen Elizabeth, a total of forty-five in all. The medal was normally awarded in silver, but a few were issued in bronze, these being without a bar or just occasionally with bars for Somaliland 1902–04 or Somaliland 1908–10. The bronze issues are, therefore, scarce, as indeed are all issues with the head of George V, a factor which has probably escaped the notice of the majority of collectors when they consider values.

(For a detailed study of the campaigns and the medal, see *Africa General Service Medals* by R. B. Magor

137 b

137 jj

137 ff

| | | 1 *Royal Navy* | 2 *British Regiments* | 3 *African & Indian Regiments* |
|---|---|---|---|---|
| a | No bar (bronze) | —— | —— | £175 |
| b | N. Nigeria 1902 | —— | —— | £125 |
| c | N. Nigeria 1903 | —— | —— | £85 |
| d | N. Nigeria 1903 (bronze) | —— | —— | £225 |
| e | N. Nigeria 1903–04 | —— | —— | £275 |
| f | N. Nigeria 1904 | —— | —— | £200 |
| g | N. Nigeria 1906 | —— | —— | £225 |
| h | S. Nigeria | —— | —— | £425 |
| i | S. Nigeria 1902 | —— | —— | £250 |
| j | S. Nigeria 1902–03 | —— | —— | £250 |
| k | S. Nigeria 1903 | —— | —— | £175 |
| l | S. Nigeria 1903–04 | —— | —— | £400 |

| | | 1 *Royal Navy* | 2 *British Regiments* | 3 *African & Indian Regiments* |
|---|---|---|---|---|
| m | S. Nigeria 1904 | — | — | £140 |
| n | S. Nigeria 1904–05 | — | — | £350 |
| o | S. Nigeria 1905 | — | — | £800 |
| p | S. Nigeria 1905–06 | — | — | £200 |
| q | Nigeria 1918 | — | — | £125 |
| r | E. Africa 1902 | — | — | £850 |
| s | E. Africa 1904 | — | — | £700 |
| t | E. Africa 1905 | — | — | £300 |
| u | E. Africa 1906 | — | — | £475 |
| v | E. Africa 1913 | — | — | £450 |
| w | E. Africa 1913–14 | — | — | £400 |
| x | E. Africa 1914 | — | — | £450 |
| y | E. Africa 1915 | — | — | £450 |
| z | E. Africa 1918 | — | — | £125 |
| aa | W. Africa 1906 | — | — | £225 |
| bb | W. Africa 1908 | — | — | £600 |
| cc | W. Africa 1909–10 | — | — | £325 |
| dd | Somaliland 1901 | — | — | £325 |
| ee | Somaliland 1901 (bronze) | — | — | £300 |
| ff | Somaliland 1902–04 | £75 | £75 | £55 |
| gg | Somaliland 1902–04 (bronze) | — | — | £70 |
| hh | Somaliland 1908–10 | £85 | — | £80 |
| ii | Somaliland 1908–10 (bronze) | — | — | £90 |
| jj | Somaliland 1920 (RAF £250) | £120 | — | £80 |
| kk | Jidballi (not awarded singly—with Somaliland 1902–04) | — | £125 | £90 |
| ll | Uganda 1900 | — | — | £140 |
| mm | B.C.A. 1899–90 | — | — | £150 |
| nn | Jubaland | £175 | — | £100 |
| oo | Jubaland (bronze) | — | — | £225 |
| pp | Jubaland 1917–18 | — | — | £325 |
| qq | Jubaland 1917–18 (bronze) | — | — | £250 |
| rr | Gambia | £450 | — | £300 |
| ss | Aro 1901–02 | £300 | — | £175 |
| tt | Lango 1901 | — | — | £300 |
| uu | Kissi 1905 | — | — | £375 |
| vv | Nandi 1905–06 | — | — | £80 |
| ww | Shimber Berris 1914–15 | — | — | £130 |
| xx | Nyasaland 1915 | — | — | £140 |
| yy | Kenya (RAF £75) | £95 | £60 | £110 |
| zz | 2 bars common combination | £100 | £125 | £90 |
| aaa | 2 bars scarce combination | — | — | £450 |
| bbb | 3 bars scarce combination | — | — | £475 |
| ccc | 4 bars scarce combination | — | — | £500 |
| ddd | 5 bars scarce combination | — | — | £525 |
| eee | 6 bars scarce combination | — | — | £550 |

*'British Regiments' values have only been placed against those bars where at least one British regiment was present in some force*

## 138 The Imperial East Africa Company's Medal 1900–03

This is the rarest of the medals awarded by the trading companies, such as the British South Africa, Royal Niger and the British North Borneo Company. The medals were frequently named, and in the main were awarded for active services in the general area of Uganda at the turn of the nineteenth century. It would appear that the medals which were all in silver were awarded with an ornamental scroll suspender or a simple ring suspender.

£60

138

138 (*reverse*)

139 b

## 139 The Tibet Medal 1903–04

It was the desire of the British Government to extend trading relations with Tibet, partly for reasons of commerce, but partly to counter the growing Russian influence in the area. A trade mission under Colonel Younghusband was sent by the Indian Government to Tibet, but its progress was barred by hostile Tibetan troops. It thus became necessary to mount a punitive expedition, which eventually reached Lhassa, where a treaty was finally signed. The majority of the silver medals were awarded to Indian regiments, those to the few British regiments present being rather scarce.

| | 1 *Silver British Regiments* | 2 *Silver Indian Regiments* | 3 *Bronze Camp Followers etc* |
|---|---|---|---|
| a Without bar | £150 | £60 | £35 |
| b Bar Gyantse | £325 | £100 | £50 |

## 140 The Natal Medal 1906

The medal was issued by the Natal Government for services in operations following the Zulu uprising, which arose because of the refusal of the Zulus to pay taxes, which in turn was followed by the murder of two Natal policemen. Without the assistance of

140 b

140 b (*reverse*)

Imperial troops, the Natal Government soon organized their local units which quickly achieved the desired results. Medals to the Natal Naval Corps are particularly scarce, some two hundred only being issued. One interesting recipient was Sergeant-Major M. K. Ghandi who was later elected first national leader of the Independent State of India, having been previously responsible for guiding India towards independence. Later, in 1949, he was assassinated.

Some 10,000 medals were issued, 2000 only without a clasp, reading '1906'. The medal was only issued in silver.

a Without bar £135 b Bar 1906 £145

## 141 The India General Service Medal 1908–35

This is the fourth of the India General Service Medal series, being sanctioned by King Edward VII. Twelve different bars were issued

141 b

141 k

141 n

during the reign of Edward VII and George V. The medals with the bars North West Frontier 1908 and Abor 1911–12 were awarded both in silver *and* bronze, the remaining issues being in silver only.

The medals were struck both by the Royal Mint in London and by the Indian Government Mint in Calcutta, the only difference being a slight variation in the claw suspenders. Most of the bars are quite common, particularly when awarded to Indian soldiers, with the exception of Abor 1911–12, Mahsud 1919–20, Malabar 1921–22, Waziristan 1925 and Mohmand 1933.

| | | 1 *British Regiments* | 2 *Royal Air Force* | 3 *Native Regiments* |
|---|---|---|---|---|
| a | NW Frontier 1908 bronze | —— | —— | £35 |
| b | NW Frontier 1908 silver | £40 | —— | £25 |
| c | Abor 1911–12 bronze | —— | —— | £130 |
| d | Abor 1911–12 silver | —— | —— | £160 |
| e | Afghanistan NWF 1919 | £30 | £120 | £20 |
| f | Mahsud 1919–20 (not awarded singly, with bar Waziristan 1919–21) | £85 | £150 | £40 |
| g | Waziristan 1919–21 | £30 | £140 | £18 |
| h | Malabar 1921–22 | £75 | —— | £40 |
| i | Waziristan 1921–24 | £40 | £100 | £30 |
| j | Waziristan 1925 | —— | £350 | —— |
| k | NW Frontier 1930–31 | £80 | £85 | £22 |
| l | Burma 1930–32 | £70 | £700 | £25 |
| m | Mohmand 1933 | —— | £150 | £35 |
| n | NW Frontier 1935 | £125 | £125 | £20 |

142 f

## 142 The Khedive's Sudan Medal 1910

This medal, which is particularly scarce to British troops, was introduced by the Khedive of Egypt to replace the previous Sudan Medal (No. 123) which was awarded between 1896 and 1908. It was awarded for numerous small expeditions, mostly in the southern part of the country, between 1910 and 1922. Bars were awarded, which contained an inscription in both English and Arabic. The silver medal was issued with bars to combatant troops, and without a bar to non-combatants. The medal was also issued in bronze without a clasp to transport personnel, servants and camp followers generally.

The first issue of the medal was from 1910 until 1918, when the new Khedive changed the Arabic cypher and date.

| | | | | | |
|---|---|---|---|---|---|
| a | Silver without bar, 1st issue | £85 | m | Fasher | £140 |
| b | Silver without bar, 2nd issue | £85 | n | Lau Nuer | £150 |
| c | Bronze without bar, 1st issue | £100 | o | Nyima 1917–18 | £120 |
| d | Bronze without bar, 2nd issue | £100 | p | Atwot 1918 | £110 |
| e | Atwot | £110 | q | Garjak Nuer | £120 |
| f | S. Kordofan 1910 | £125 | r | Aliab Dinka | £200 |
| g | Sudan 1912 | £150 | s | Nyala | £140 |
| h | Zeeraf 1913–14 | £170 | t | Darfur 1921 | £160 |
| i | Mandal | £130 | u | 2 bars | £140 |
| j | Miri | £180 | v | 3 bars | £170 |
| k | Mongalla 1915–16 | £150 | w | 4 bars | £200 |
| l | Darfur 1916 | £120 | x | 5 bars | £240 |

*All unnamed as issued*

## 143 The 1914 and 1914–15 Stars

These stars, of which there are three distinct issues, were the first of several medals issued to commemorate the holocaust of the First World War. The first star, approved in 1917, was the 1914 Star for award to all those who had served in France and Belgium, on the strength of a unit, between 5th August and midnight on 22nd/23rd November 1914; fewer than 400,000 were issued. In 1919, the King sanctioned the award of a bar to the previously issued 1914 Star to those who had actually been under fire which came to be known as 'The Mons Star'.

The majority of the recipients of the 1914 Star would have been the pre-war regular Army, known as 'The Old Contemptibles', a

143 b

143 d

term that the German Emperor Kaiser Wilhelm used when referring to the small but professional British Army.

The third type of star is known as the 1914–15 Star, which is identical to the 1914 Star except that the central scroll carries the dates 1914–15 instead of 5 Aug.–22 Nov. 1914. This 1914–15 Star was awarded to those who saw service in any theatre of war between 5th August 1914 and 31st December 1915, except, of course, those who had previously qualified for the 1914 Stars. The plain reverses are all inscribed and the variety of units, both British and Commonwealth, is immense, which makes the collecting and study of these a particularly interesting one for the younger collector.

We therefore have three different issues, the 1914 Star, 1914 Star with bar (known as the Mons Star) and the 1914–15 Star.

| | | |
|---|---|---|
| a | 1914 Star | £14 |
| b | 1914 Star with 'Mons' bar, Army | £20 |
| c | 1914 Star with 'Mons' bar, RNVR Btns | £30 |
| d | 1914–15 Star | £4 |

144
(*reverse*)

## 144 The British War Medal 1914–20

Issued in both silver and bronze to commemorate some of the most terrible battles ever known resulting in astronomical casualties. Some 6,500,000 medals in silver and 110,000 in bronze were issued, the latter awarded mostly to Chinese, Maltese and other native labour corps.

Originally, it was intended to award bars to commemorate participation in the different battles; seventy-nine were suggested by the Army and sixty-eight by the Navy but, due to the huge number of medals authorized, the project of issuing bars had to be abandoned on account of the immense expense. However, the Naval bars were actually authorized and, although they were not issued, some recipients had their miniatures made so as to include bars.

The medal was also awarded for post-First World War service in Russia, covering the period 1919–20 and for mine clearance in the North Sea up until the end of November 1919.

a Silver £13 b Bronze £30

## 145 The Mercantile Marine War Medal 1914–18

Awarded in bronze by the Board of Trade to members of the Mercantile Marine who had undertaken one or more voyages through a war or danger zone. Unlike the earlier Merchant Navy medals issued for the third China and Boer Wars (No. 134) which were given in silver to officers only, this was awarded to all ranks in bronze; just over 133,000 medals were issued. The riband is interesting in that it represents the steaming lights of a ship under way.

£13

144

## 146 The Victory Medal 1914–18

146

Issued in bronze to all those who had received the 1914 or 1914/15 Stars, and to most of those who were awarded the British War Medal—it was never awarded by itself. Nearly six million medals were issued in all, those being Mentioned in Despatches were allowed to wear an oak leaf on the riband. The reverse inscription of those issued by the South African Government is in both English and Afrikaans.

The medal is often called 'the Allied Victory Medal', as the same basic design and riband were adopted by Belgium, Brazil (an extremely rare issue), Cuba, Czechoslovakia, France, Greece, Italy, Japan, Portugal, Roumania, Siam, the Union of South Africa and the USA. In the case of Japan, the winged figure of Victory which appeared on the obverse, was replaced by a warrior holding a spear; the USA issue often contains battle bars. Collectors will find it an interesting study to collect those issued by all the allies, but it is unlikely that they will come across one awarded by Brazil.

To avoid controversy, the riband adopted included all the colours of the rainbow in a shaded and watered effect.

| | | | | | |
|---|---|---|---|---|---|
| a | United Kingdom | £1 | h | Italy | £5 |
| b | Belgium | £5 | i | Japan | £40 |
| c | Brazil | £500 | j | Portugal | £35 |
| d | Cuba | £85 | k | Roumania | £30 |
| e | Czechoslovakia | £30 | l | Siam | £50 |
| f | France | £5 | m | S. Africa | £15 |
| g | Greece | £30 | n | USA (without bar) | £5 |

## 147 The Territorial Force War Medal 1914–19

As only 34,000 medals were issued to the Territorials, this makes the medal the rarest of the five medals issued to cover the First World War. The bronze medal was awarded to all members of the Territorial Force, including nursing sisters, who were members of

145 (*reverse*)

145

the service on 4th August 1914 and who had completed four years' service before that date. In addition, they must have:

1. undertaken on or before 30th September 1914 to serve outside the UK;
2. to have actually served outside the UK between 4th August 1914 and 11th November 1918; and
3. been eligible for either the 1914 or 1914–15 Stars.

£30

## 148 The Naval General Service Medal 1915–64

This is the second Naval General Service Medal to have been issued since medals were first introduced, the earlier one being the

148 e

148 j

148 a

149 b

one awarded predominantly for the Napoleonic Wars from 1793 (No 81).

The medal was issued with the obverse effigies of Kings George V and VI and also Queen Elizabeth II. The medal was instituted to avoid having to issue a separate medal for the numerous operations in which the Royal Navy and Royal Marines were involved, excluding the general areas of Africa and India, these regions already being covered by the Africa (1902) and Indian Service (1908) Medals.

The medal covers a fascinating range of different actions, some of the bars being particularly rare. The medals issued with any of the first three bars contained the name of the recipient's ship, but this interesting collecting aspect lapsed until the recent issue of the Falkland Islands Medal.

The bar for Yangtze 1949 is perhaps the best-known incident for which the medal was given. HMS *Amethyst* was ordered up the River Yangtze to relieve HMS *Consort* and to take supplies to the British Embassy. On her way up she was heavily shelled by the Chinese Communist forces and temporarily driven ashore with seventeen killed and ten wounded. The result was that the British had to send the cruiser HMS *London*, the frigate *Black Swan* and HMS *Consort* to relieve her, but they failed, and as the supplies of the *Amethyst* were running very low after a period of one hundred days' detention with the crew on half-rations, the relief captain, Lt-Cdr Kerans, RN, decided to make a dash downriver past the enemy strong points, which resulted in the famous signal being sent by *Amethyst*, 'Have rejoined the fleet. No damage or casualties. God save the King.'

Due to the vastly different types of operations which this medal covers, especially the post-Second World War, and the wide combination of bars that is available, the medal will undoubtedly become a very cherished collectors' piece in the years to come.

| | | | | | |
|---|---|---|---|---|---|
| a | Persian Gulf 1909–14 | £75 | k | Yangtze 1949 to HMS *Amethyst* | £750 |
| b | Iraq 1919–20 | £650 | l | Yangtze to other ships | £425 |
| c | NW Persia 1920 | £900 | m | Bomb and mine clearance 1945–53 | £350 |
| d | NW Persia 1919–20 | £900 | n | Bomb and mine clearance Mediterranean | £1000 |
| e | Palestine 1936–39 | £50 | o | Cyprus | £35 |
| f | SE Asia 1945–46 | £100 | p | Near East | £50 |
| g | Minesweeping 1945–51 | £90 | q | Arabian Peninsula | £80 |
| h | Palestine 1945–48 | £40 | r | Brunei | £120 |
| i | Malaya George VI | £45 | | | |
| j | Malaya E.IIR. | £45 | | | |

## 149 The General Service Medal 1918–64

Awarded to the Army and Royal Air Force (the Navy's General Service Medal was already in existence, No 148) for the numerous actions which fell short of actual war. This medal did not cover service in Africa or India, services in these areas were covered by the Africa G.S. 1902 and Indian G.S. 1908 Medals. As with the Naval equivalent, this medal covers a very wide and interesting range of actions or campaigns in many different parts of the world. Many post-Second World War operations are commemorated by bars such as Malaya, Cyprus, Egypt, Aden and Brunei—Brunei being particularly scarce. In all, sixteen different bars were issued, the majority are quite common with the exception of Southern Desert, Iraq, Northern Kurdistan, the two bomb and mine clearance bars and Brunei.

149 g 149 l 149 c

| | | 1 *British Regiments* | 2 *Royal Air Force* | 3 *Indian & Local Regiments* |
|---|---|---|---|---|
| a | S. Persia | —— | £400 | £40 |
| b | Kurdistan | £45 | £275 | £35 |
| c | Iraq | £40 | £200 | £35 |
| d | NW Persia | £60 | £275 | £45 |
| e | Southern Desert, Iraq | —— | £300 | —— |
| f | Northern Kurdistan | —— | £275 | £100 |
| g | Palestine (1936–39) | £24 | £50 | £20 |
| h | Bomb and Mine Clearance 1945–49 | £250 | £250 | —— |
| i | Bomb and Mine Clearance 1945–56 | £300 | £300 | —— |
| j | Palestine 1945–48 | £20 | £30 | £20 |
| k | Malaya (George VI obverse) | £18 | £20 | £18 |
| l | Malaya (E.IIR. obverse) | £18 | £20 | £18 |
| m | SE Asia 1945–46 | £45 | £50 | £20 |
| n | Cyprus | £18 | £20 | —— |
| o | Near East | £50 | £60 | —— |
| p | Arabian Peninsula | £30 | £35 | —— |
| q | Brunei | £100 | —— | £80 |

## 150 The India General Service Medal 1936–39

This medal, the fifth and last medal in the India General Service series, was introduced to replace the issue covering the period 1908–35, the accession of King George VI to the throne providing a convenient time in which to change the medal. The medal covered the shortest period of time in the whole of the Indian series, for it was terminated in 1939 by the outbreak of the Second World War after which, with the partition of the Indian subcontinent, the issue of further medals became null and void.

There were two issues or strikings, one by the Royal Mint and the other by the Mint in Calcutta; the medal was never awarded without a bar.

150 a

150 a (*reverse*)

| | 1 *Royal Mint Issue to British Troops* | 2 *Calcutta Issue to Native Troops* |
|---|---|---|
| a NW Frontier 1936–37 | £55 | £20 |
| b NW Frontier 1937–39 | £60 | £25 |
| c 2 bars | £90 | £30 |

## 151 The Second World War Campaign Stars 1939–45

There were eight different campaign stars which were almost identical in design—six-pointed stars with the crowned cypher of King George VI in the centre. The central cypher is partly surrounded by the name of the appropriate campaign, which reads either 1939–45, Atlantic, Air Crew Europe, Africa, Pacific, Burma, Italy or France/Germany. The stars were made of a copper-zinc alloy and, unlike the medals of the First World War, were unnamed.

It was decreed that the maximum number of stars that could be earned by any one man or woman was five, and those who qualified for more received a clasp to the riband of an associated star. Only one clasp to a riband was allowed. Therefore, the stars could carry the following bars:

1. 1939/45 (Battle of Britain);
2. Atlantic (Air Crew Europe *or* France and Germany);
3. Air Crew Europe (Atlantic *or* France and Germany);
4. Africa (North Africa 1942–43—issue to Naval forces *or* 8th Army *or* 1st Army);
5. Pacific (Burma);
6. Burma (Pacific);
7. Italy (no bars issued);
8. France and Germany (Atlantic *or* Air Crew Europe).

151 a

151 c 151 d 151 e

151 f 151 g 151 h

When ribands only are worn, the additional bar that might have been earned by a recipient is represented by a silver rosette, but the Battle of Britain clasp was represented by a gold-plated rosette. All the ribands are symbolic, it being said that these were designed by King George VI. The riband of the 1939–45 Star represents the three forces: the Atlantic riband represents the sea, incidentally the symbolism of this riband was also adopted for the recent South Atlantic Medal; the Air Crew Europe riband represents the sky by a blue stripe, yellow for the search-lights and black for night-time flying; the Africa riband basically represents the desert, the central broad stripe of red representing the major effort by the Army, flanked by lesser stripes of dark blue and light blue for the Navy and Air Force. The Pacific riband represents in the centre the jungle, with a narrow yellow stripe for the beaches, flanked by narrow stripes of dark blue for the Navy and light blue for the Air Force, and on each edge rather wider stripes of red represent the Army. The central red stripe incorporated in the Burma riband represents the Commonwealth forces and the orange stripes the sun. The Italian riband represents the colours of the Italian State flag, while the France and Germany star represents the colours from the French and Dutch flags.

151 i

| | | | | | |
|---|---|---|---|---|---|
| a | 1939–45 Star | £3 | d | Air Crew Europe | £50 |
| b | 1939–45 Star with Battle of Britain clasp *in a group with an officially named medal* | £50 | e | Africa | £3 |
| | | | f | Pacific | £8 |
| | | | g | Burma | £5 |
| | | | h | Italy | £3 |
| | | | i | France & Germany | £8 |
| c | Atlantic Star | £8 | | | |

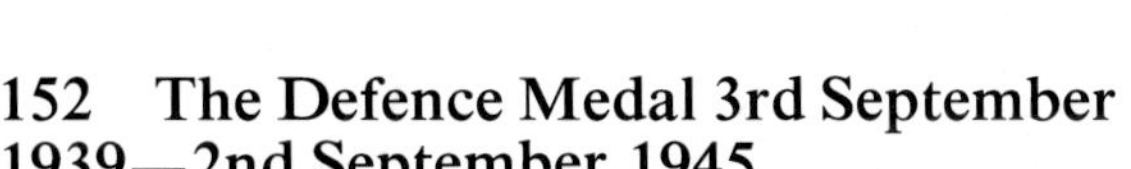

## 152 The Defence Medal 3rd September 1939—2nd September 1945

As this medal was also awarded to a large number of civilians who formed part of recognized defence units, such as the Home Guard or Civil Defence, the medal is the commonest of the Second World War series. The medal was issued unnamed in cupro-nickel, although the Canadian issue was made in silver. The riband is symbolic of the British Isles, which is represented by green, the orange colour represents the bombing (fires) of the UK that took place, and the black the black-out.

152

| | | | |
|---|---|---|---|
| a | Cupro-nickel £4 | b | Silver £12 |

## 153 The War Medal 3rd September 1939—2nd September 1945

This medal was awarded to all full-time personnel of the armed forces wherever they were serving, providing that they had served for at least twenty-eight days, irrespective of whether they were operational or non-operational. As with the Defence Medal, this was awarded unnamed in cupro-nickel, although the Canadian issues were in silver. The cupro-nickel medals issued to the South African and Australian troops were named with the recipients' number and name. Due to the large numbers issued, the medal is one of the least expensive of the whole Second World War series.

| | | |
|---|---|---|
| a | Cupro-nickel | £2 |
| b | Cupro-nickel named to Australian & S. African forces | £4 |
| c | Silver | £12 |

153

## 154 The Indian Service Medal 1939–45

Awarded to officers and men of the Indian forces for three years' non-operational service in India or elsewhere and issued unnamed in cupro-nickel. It was frequently awarded in conjunction with the Campaign Stars and the War Medal, but never with the Defence

Medal. This, incidentally, was the last of the series of medals, which covered a period of almost one hundred and fifty years, awarded in conjunction with India.

£7

154 155 b

## 155 The Canadian Volunteer Service Medal 1939–47

Authorized as early as 1943 and issued unnamed in silver for eighteen months' voluntary service in the Canadian forces. Those who served overseas were entitled to wear a bar on the riband which depicted a maple leaf.

a Without bar £13 b With bar £14

156

## 156 The South African Service Medal 1939–45

Instituted in 1943 for award to the armed forces of South Africa for service during the Second World War, both at home and abroad. The medals were made in silver and officially named, and issued to all full-time service members of the Union forces for a period of thirty days' service or more in South Africa. One interesting aspect is that those with the prefix 'N' indicate a native recipient, and 'C' a coloured recipient.

£15

## 157 The South African Medal for War Service 1939–46

Awarded in silver to both men and women, the main qualification being two years' service in any official voluntary organization in South Africa or elsewhere—service *had* to be unpaid and voluntary. The medal could not be awarded with the previous South African War Service Medal (No 156). Only 17,000 were awarded so the medal is scarce by Second World War standards.

£45

157

## 158 The Australian Service Medal 1939–45

Awarded to members of the Australian forces, being authorized rather late, in December 1949. The medal was awarded in cupronickel, but was named. The prefix before the number indicates the state in which the recipient enlisted. The recipients had to serve for eighteen months overseas, or do three years' service at home.

£7

158

159

## 159 The New Zealand War Service Medal 1939–45

Issued to all members of the New Zealand forces during the Second World War, including many reserve and home service units. Awarded in cupro-nickel and issued unnamed.

£10

## 160 The Southern Rhodesia War Service Medal 1939–45

This scarce medal was awarded to all those who served in Southern Rhodesia during the Second World War, but it was not awarded to those who qualified for an overseas campaign star or medal and, as very many Rhodesians served overseas, only 1700 medals were issued. The medals were in cupro-nickel and were issued unnamed.

£90

161 d

161 d

## 161 The Korea Medal 1950–53

Awarded to members of both the British and Commonwealth forces who took part in the operations in Korea.

Following the conclusion of the Second World War, the Korean peninsula was divided into two countries; the northern part was under Communist control and the southern came under American influence or protection. After a time, the controlling power in the south withdrew its forces which resulted in the north attacking the south, thus causing the United Nations to intervene with forces drawn from a great variety of different countries, but the USA, Great Britain and the Commonwealth made the most sizeable contributions. The British and Commonwealth forces were frequently very heavily engaged.

The most sought-after medals in this series are those to men of the Gloucester Regiment, who took part in the epic battle of the Imjim River. The medals were in cupro-nickel, although those issued by Canada were in silver, with the obverse legend incorporating the word 'Canada'. The Union of South Africa and Rhodesia issued their own special medals, which are quite scarce on the market.

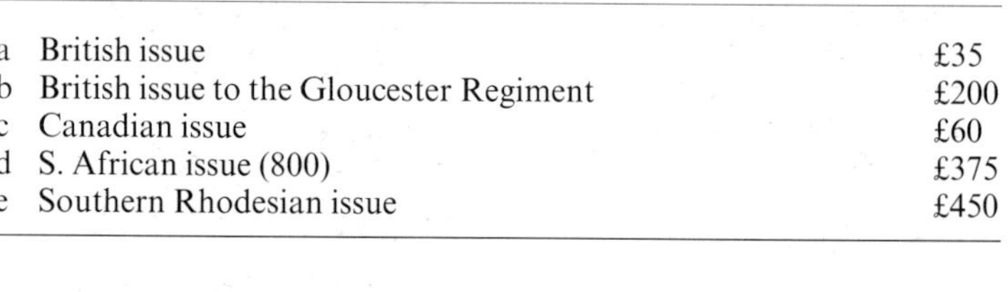

| | | |
|---|---|---|
| a | British issue | £35 |
| b | British issue to the Gloucester Regiment | £200 |
| c | Canadian issue | £60 |
| d | S. African issue (800) | £375 |
| e | Southern Rhodesian issue | £450 |

## 162 The United Nations Korea Medal 1950–53

This bronze medal was awarded by the United Nations to all those who served in the UN forces during the Korean war. It was awarded to all those who held the British Medal and to those who served in Korea after the armistice in 1953. The medal was issued unnamed, except those to Canadians, which were named in small block capitals. Various types were issued to the different contingents, the reverse naming appearing in the language of the contingent concerned.

162 a

| | | | | | |
|---|---|---|---|---|---|
| a | English unnamed | £10 | g | Greek | £60 |
| b | English named to Canadians | £20 | h | Italian | £100 |
| c | Amharic (Ethiopia) | £70 | i | Koreans | £20 |
| d | Dutch | £50 | j | Spanish | £80 |
| e | Flemish (Belgium) | £30 | k | Tagalog (Philippines) | £50 |
| f | French | £20 | l | Thai | £60 |
| | | | m | Turkish | £35 |

## 163 The General Service Medal 1962–

This medal was introduced to replace the Naval General Service Medal of 1915 and the General Service Medal (Army and RAF) 1918. These two medals had been issued over a long period and it was decided to issue a uniform medal to all three forces when the Ministry of Defence assumed unified control of all three forces. To date, seven bars have been issued: Borneo, (24th December 1962 — 11th August 1966) for service against rebel forces in Sabah, Sarawak and Brunei; Radfan (25th April — 31st July) for service in the South Arabian Federation; South Arabia (1st August — 30th November 1967) for supporting the local government against insurgent forces; Malay Peninsula (17th August 1964 — 11th August 1966) for efforts during the confrontation with Indonesia; South Vietnam (24th September 1962 — 29th May 1964) for award to Australian forces only as the UK was not at war in South Vietnam; Northern Ireland (from August 1969) for participation in peace-keeping and police duties, the clasp is still being awarded; and Dhofar (1969–76) for supporting the Sultan of Oman's forces in their operations against the Communist forces operating from South Yemen.

Five bars seem to have been the maximum issued so far to any one medal and, as can be seen from the price list below, some bars are particularly scarce. In some cases medals are scarce to one force and more common to others.

163 h (*reverse*) 163 h

| | | |
|---|---|---|
| a | Borneo | £20 |
| b | Radfan | £50 |
| c | S. Arabia | £25 |
| d | Malay Peninsula | £25 |
| e | S. Vietnam | £275 |
| f | Northern Ireland | £18 |
| g | Dhofar | £155 |

| | | 1 *Excluding Dhofar* | 2 *Including Dhofar* |
|---|---|---|---|
| h | 2 bars | £30 | £180 |
| i | 3 bars | £50 | £200 |
| j | 4 bars | £125 | £300 |

*Multiple bars (above) exclude S. Vietnam*

## 164 The United Nations Emergency Force Medal 1956–67

Awarded to those that served with the Emergency Force which followed the brief war between Israel and Egypt. The objective of the Force was to organize patrols and enforce peace on the Israeli/Egyptian border. The medals were issued to troops from Brazil, Canada, Columbia, Denmark, Finland, Indonesia, Norway, Sweden and Yugoslavia.

£20

## 165 The Vietnam Medals 1964

British forces were not involved in this war, the medals being issued to the armed forces and accredited relief societies of Australia and New Zealand, and announced in the Government of Australia's *Gazette* on 4th July 1968 and the New Zealand *Gazette* on 8th August 1968. Approximately 18,000 medals were issued to the Australian forces and 4000 to the forces of New Zealand. The riband represents the three services, namely dark blue, light blue and red, together with the national colours of South Vietnam.

165 a 165 b

The Government of Vietnam also issued an award to the recipients of the above-mentioned medal in the same way as the United Nations issued their bronze medal for Korea. The medals issued by Vietnam were rather crudely manufactured and unnamed and, as a result, the Australian Government manufactured their own superior version, which were all named.

| | | |
|---|---|---|
| a | Australian and New Zealand issue | £50 |
| b | S. Vietnam issue (named to Commonwealth forces) | £14 |

## 166 The South Atlantic Medal 2nd April 1982

Struck in cupro-nickel with a straight bar which swivels—the first cupro medal to do so—named to recipients and awarded to those who were involved in regaining possession of the Falkland Islands and South Georgia from Argentina. Those that served for at least one day in the Falklands, etc, or in the South Atlantic south of sixty-five degrees south, or in any operational aircraft south of Ascension Island were awarded a distinguishing rosette worn on the riband of the medal or on the riband only when worn without the medal. Others, who served outside these areas, had to serve for thirty days and received the medal without rosette.

166 b

| | | | | | |
|---|---|---|---|---|---|
| a | Medal | £140 | b | Medal with rosette | £160 |

## 167 The United Nations Medals

The United Nations have over a period of years issued many medals in addition to those for Korea. All the medals are of the same design but were awarded with different ribands for the different areas where the troops were involved. Some of the issues are rather scarce and these *should* command a higher price but this is defeated as it would be easy for a standard medal to have a riband fitted to represent a scarce issue—ribands are freely available for a few pence. Those issued to date cover:

The Congo 1960–64; Truce Supervisory Organisation (Israel/Arab area); The Observer Group in the Lebanon 1958; The Temporary Executive Authority 1962 (Netherlands, New Guinea/Indonesia); Military Observer Group in India and Pakistan (1949– ); India and Pakistan Observer Mission (1965–66); Yemen Observation Mission (1963–64); Cyprus (1964– ); Emergency Force (1973– ); Disengagement Force (1974– ); Interim Force on Lebanon (1978– ). General Service Medal.

*All valued at* £20

*However*, a special medal was issued for services between 1956–67 with the UN Emergency Force (Israel/Egypt). This medal had 'UNEF' on the obverse as opposed to the standard medal which contained 'UN'.

£35

167

# Miscellaneous Medals

## 168 The Polar Medal 1818–

Ever since the spice trade commenced with the Far East, man's endeavours were directed towards finding a north-west passage north of Canada so as to considerably shorten the journey. It was this need to find such a passage which resulted in numerous voyages of polar exploration.

The first Polar Medal was authorized in 1857, covering the period 1818–55, and was awarded to all ranks engaged in certain expeditions, including the search for the lost Franklin expedition of 1845–48. This series of medals, which are still being awarded today, is a fascinating series representing extreme human endeavour against an enemy as old as time, namely the atrocious weather and conditions that existed and still exist in both the Arctic and the Antarctic. The second series of medals were those covering the period 1875–76. These and the earlier first issue were in silver, while the third issue, which is currently being awarded, was introduced in 1904 in both silver and bronze, with dated bars covering the period(s) of service. The first recipients of the third 1904 issue were awarded to Captain Scott's first expedition to the Antarctic, followed by Sir Ernest Shackleton's expedition of 1907 and then Scott's last fateful expedition of 1910–13. From that date, medals have been issued on a fairly regular basis, being awarded to the ever increasing numbers of expeditions and

168

168 (2)

scientific bases that have been set up and are constantly manned in the Antarctic.

Since 1939 the third 1904 issue has only been awarded in silver. Needless to say, Polar Medals are scarce and quite valuable, with the possible exception of those awarded for the first expedition of 1818–55.

For a complete study of the expeditions covered by the Polar Medals and a list of the recipients, readers are recommended to *The White Ribbon* by N. W. Poulsom.

| | | |
|---|---|---|
| a | Arctic 1818–55 (*unnamed*) | £160 |
| | *The above is the only one in the series, issued unnamed.* | |
| b | *Privately engraved medals . . .* | £220 |
| c | Arctic 1875–76 | £450 |
| d | Polar Medal 1904. | |
| | 1 Bronze, from | £400 |
| | 2 Silver, from | £500 |

## 169 The Naval Engineers Medal 1842–46

This medal, instituted in 1842 and abolished in 1846, was intended to reward 'Engineers of the First Class Service in Her Majesty's Navy, who by their good conduct and ability deserve some special mark of notice.' Only eight medals were awarded before its abolition, these being for services such as that of Mr James Urquhart, who was serving aboard HMSV *Columbia*, for inventing a tide motor. The idea was that the incoming tide exerted pressure on a device suspended below a pier, this device revolved a series of gear wheels linked to an electric generator and, at the turn of the tide, a link came into operation so that the outgoing tide also performed the same duty. Today, we are still experimenting with such devices to generate electricity.

| | | | |
|---|---|---|---|
| a Named | £950 | b Specimen | £125 |

169

169 (*reverse*)

## 170 The King Edward VII Medal for Science, Art and Music

A very scarce silver medal introduced by Edward VII in 1904 in recognition of distinguished services to the arts, but discontinued in 1906. The obverse was unusual in that it contained the conjoint busts of Edward and Queen Alexandra.

£450

## 171 The Indian Title Badges

Introduced by the King Emperor George V at the coronation or durbar at Delhi in December 1911. They were awarded in three classes to civilians and to the Viceroy's commissioned officers of the Indian Army for faithful service or acts of public welfare.

A recipient had to be awarded the lowest grade before advancing to a senior grade, and if he received promotion or, in other words, two decorations, only the senior award and title were used. The design of the badge was the same for all three classes but not the wording. The badges took precedence after all British and Indian orders and decorations but came immediately before war medals.

The titles of the different classes were as follows:

| | | |
|---|---|---|
| a | *1st Class*—'Diwan Bahadur' for Moslems<br>'Sardar Bahadur' for Hindus | £60 |
| b | *2nd Class*—'Khan Bahadur' for Moslems<br>'Rai' or 'Rao Bahadur' for Hindus | £40 |
| c | *3rd Class*—'Khan Sahib' for Moslems<br>'Rai' or 'Rao Sahib' for Hindus | £30 |

171c

172 b

## 172 The Indian Army Recruiting Badges

Awarded for outstanding recruiting services during the First and Second World Wars.

a George V £40 b George VI £50

## 173 The Order of the League of Mercy

Appointments to the Order are approved and sanctioned by the Sovereign upon the recommendation of the Grand President of the League of Mercy. Given as a reward for distinguished personal service on behalf of the League in assisting hospitals with the relief of suffering, poverty or distress. They were awarded to ladies or gentlemen who had graciously rendered services to the League.

The award was allowed to be worn in uniform.

£45

173

## 174 The Union of South Africa Medal 1910

Distributed in silver, sometimes found named. Awarded to all Government officials and selected servicemen who participated in the ceremonies commemorating the foundation of the Union in 1910.

a Named £275 b Unnamed £200

175

175
(*reverse*)

## 175 The Sultan of Zanzibar's Medal

Awarded to the Sultan's forces who were under the command of Lt Lloyd Matthew, RN, the Naval Lieutenant being promoted to Brigadier General, which is probably a record regarding promotion! The unusual feature of this unnamed medal, issued towards the end of the nineteenth century, was that it contained the face and bust of the Sultan; even today, many Arabic countries are rather loath to issue medals and coinage containing an effigy, which is against the teachings of Mohammed.

£80

176

## 176 HMAS *Sydney* SMS *Emden* Medal

Early on in the First World War, the Australian cruiser *Sydney* located the German light cruiser *Emden* in the Cocos Islands in the vicinity of south-west Sumatra. When the *Emden* was eventually boarded, a quantity of Mexican dollars was found. Many of these dollars were mounted as medals and given to the crew of HMAS *Sydney* to commemorate the engagement while others were sold to the general public to defray the cost of distribution to the crew. The medal, therefore, consists of a Mexican dollar piece on which a crown has been fitted, with the words '9th November 1914, HMAS *Sydney*—SMS *Emden*'. Being strictly speaking mementoes, the 'medals' were not allowed to be worn on uniform.

a £65 b (Mounted by W. Kerr of Sydney) £125

## 177 The Rhodesia Medal 1980

Awarded by the British Government in rhodium-plated cupronickel to members of the British and Commonwealth forces, to

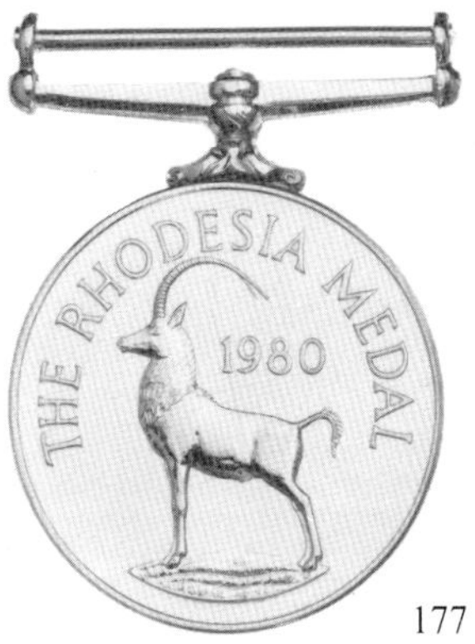


177

police and to a team of observers who were sent out to supervise and regulate the elections that took place, which resulted in the birth of present-day Zimbabwe.

£325

## 178 The King's Medal for Service in the Cause of Freedom

This unnamed silver medal was the counter-part of the First World War Allied Subjects Medal, and was awarded to civilians of foreign nationality for furthering the interest of the British Commonwealth in the Allied cause during the 1939–45 War. It is thought that some 3000 of these medals were issued. The medal is not to be confused with a similar King's medal awarded for *courage*.

£200

178

## 179 The Commonwealth Independence Medals issued since 1946

A large number of countries in the Commonwealth have gained independence since 1946 and many of them have issued commemorative medals, these being awarded to visiting officials as well as to their own Government officials, etc. Many of them are quite scarce. The medals awarded are:

| | | |
|---|---|---|
| a | Pakistan 1947 | £8 |
| b | India 1947 | £8 |
| c | Ghana 1957 (1000) | £95 |
| d | Nigeria 1960 | £25 |
| e | Sierra Leone 1961 (5660) | £50 |
| f | Jamaica 1962 (6050) | £25 |
| g | Uganda 1962 (15,000) | £40 |
| h | Malawi 1964 (1800) | £70 |
| i | Fiji 1970 | £70 |
| j | Kenya 1973 | |
| | 1 (40,000–29,775 cupro-nickel | £30 |
| | 2 10,000 gold plated | £30 |
| | 3 225 gold plated but in the form of commemorative medallions | £40 |
| k | Papua New Guinea 1975 | £50 |
| l | Zimbabwe 1980 | |
| | 1 Silver £35 2 Bronze | £25 |
| m | Gilbert and Ellis Islands 1978 | £70 |
| n | Solomon Islands | £80 |
| o | Guyana 1966 | £45 |

179 b

179d

179 h

179 i

179 k

179 n

## 180 Good Shooting Medals

The first officially issued medals for good shooting were introduced in 1869. However, long before this date, individually engraved silver medals were often issued by officers commanding not only the regular regiments, but also the hastily raised volunteer regiments during the Napoleonic period, as well as the volunteers and militia since then.

If one considers that the main object of a serviceman in action has always been to shoot the opposition before being shot at himself, perhaps it is quite natural that medals would have been issued for good shooting so as to encourage this art. However, official Government issues since 1869 have always been awarded very sparingly.

The Royal Navy did not institute a medal until 1903 and it was discontinued in 1914, probably on the assumption that the Navy would be given plenty of live practice against the enemy! The Army's award, introduced in 1869, was discontinued as early as 1882, and revised in 1923. The Air Force's award was introduced as late as 1953, and was known as 'The Queen's Medal for Champion Shots of the Air Force'.

| | | |
|---|---|---|
| a | **Naval Good Shooting Medal 1903–14** | |
| | 1 Edward VII £120 2 George V | £175 |
| b | **Queen's Medal for Champion Shots of the RN and RM** | £400 |
| c | **Queen's Medal for Champion Shots of the New Zealand Forces 1955** | £425 |
| d | **Army Best Shot Medal** | |
| | 1 Victoria, issued 1869–82 | £275 |
| | 2 George V, issued 1923–36 | £325 |
| | 3 George VI, issued 1937–52 | £350 |
| | 4 E.IIR., issued 1953 | £350 |
| e | **Queen's Medal for Champion Shots of the Air Force 1953** | £575 |

## 181 Jubilee and Coronations Medals, etc 1887–1977

Ever since the coronation of Kind Edward VII in 1547 and up to the coronation of King George VI in 1937, the Royal Mint has always struck official commemorative medallions which were for general sale to the public, but these were not designed for wear. Since Queen Victoria's fiftieth jubilee in 1887, medals have been struck for wear with ribands, these being issued to members of the Royal Family, members of the Royal Household, ministers, officers of state, official guests from home and overseas, Government officials, civil servants, selected officers and warrant officers, non-commissioned officers and men of the services as well as the police forces. They were also issued to persons in the service of the Crown, both in the UK and throughout the Commonwealth, and were awarded to lord mayors, mayors, provosts, local Government officers, and to many others holding official positions on duty in Westminster Abbey at the coronation, and to those who participated in the ceremony.

Not only did the medals commemorate state occasions in London but also official visits that frequently followed to Scotland, Ireland and India. Up to and including the coronation of King George V in 1911, there were special issues to different sections of the community, but from the time of the jubilee in 1935, one standard medal was issued to all. Up until the Delhi Durbar in 1911, medals were struck in gold for members of the Royal Family and principal overseas representatives, in silver to other officers and in bronze to other ranks. Since 1911, all medals have been issued in silver only. Needless to say, some of the issues especially up until 1911 are rather scarce, and as the series has been somewhat neglected by collectors to date, the price structure is probably rather lower than what one would normally expect.

181a

181a
*(reverse)*

181 b

181 f

181 c

181 d

VICTORIA

| | | | | | | | | | | |
|---|---|---|---|---|---|---|---|---|---|---|
| a | **Empress of India Medal 1877** | | | | | | | | | |
| | | 1 | Gold | £1750 | 2 | Silver | £175 | | — | |
| b | **Jubilee 1887** | | | | | | | | | |
| | | 1 | Gold | £650 | 2 | Silver | £50 | 3 | Bronze | £25 |
| c | Metropolitan Police (1400) | | | | | | | | Bronze | £14 |
| d | City of London Police (900) | | | | | | | | Bronze | £45 |
| e | Police Ambulance Service | | | | | | | | Bronze | £100 |
| f | **Jubilee 1887 with '1897' Bar** | | | | | | | | | |
| | | 1 | Gold | £850 | 2 | Silver | £85 | 3 | Bronze | £40 |
| g | Metropolitan Police | | | | | | | | Bronze | £20 |
| h | City of London Police | | | | | | | | Bronze | £55 |
| i | Police Ambulance Service | | | | | | | | Bronze | £125 |
| j | **Jubilee 1897** | | | | | | | | | |
| | | 1 | Gold (73) | £600 | 2 | Silver (3040) | £45 | 3 | Bronze (890) | £20 |
| k | Lord Mayor's Issue | | | | | | | | | |
| | | 1 | Gold (14) | £850 | 2 | Silver (512) | £125 | | — | |
| l | Metropolitan Police | | | | | | | | Bronze | £12 |
| m | City of London Police | | | | | | | | Bronze | £35 |
| n | Police Ambulance Service | | | | | | | | Bronze | £80 |
| o | St John's Ambulance Brigade | | | | | | | | Bronze | £80 |
| p | LCC Metropolitan Fire Brigade | | | | | | | | Bronze | £100 |
| q | **Visit to Ireland 1900** (2285) | | | | | | | | Bronze | £60 |

181 j

181 k

181 l

181 m

181 o

181 p

181 q

## EDWARD VII

| | | | | | | | |
|---|---|---|---|---|---|---|---|
| r | **Coronation 1902** | 1 | Silver (3493) | £40 | 2 | Bronze (6054) | £30 |
| s | Lord Mayor's Issue | | Silver | £130 | | | |
| t | Metropolitan Police | 1 | Silver | £200 | 2 | Bronze | £15 |
| u | City of London Police | 1 | Silver | £250 | 2 | Bronze | £45 |
| v | LCC Metropolitan Fire Brigade | 1 | Silver | £275 | 2 | Bronze | £45 |
| w | St John's Ambulance Brigade | 1 | Silver | £300 | 2 | Bronze | £50 |
| x | County and Borough Police | 1 | Silver | £275 | 2 | Bronze | £60 |
| y | Police Ambulance Service | 1 | Silver | £300 | 2 | Bronze | £70 |
| z | **Delhi Durbar 1903**<br>1 Gold (140) £800 | 2 | Silver (2570) | £100 | | —— | |
| aa | **Visit to Scotland 1903** Police | | —— | | | (3000) Bronze | £60 |
| bb | **Visit to Ireland 1903** | | —— | | | (7760) Bronze | £60 |

181 r

181 r
(*reverse*)

181 s

181 s (*reverse*)

181 t

181 u

181 v

181 w

181 y

181 z

181 aa

181 bb

## GEORGE V

| | | | |
|---|---|---|---|
| cc | **Coronation 1911** (15,900), Silver | | £22 |
| dd | as above but with 'Delhi' clasp, Silver | | £225 |
| ee | City of London Police (134), Silver | | £120 |
| ff | Metropolitan Police, Silver | | £25 |
| gg | County and Borough Police, Silver | | £65 |
| hh | London Fire Brigade, Silver | | £85 |
| ii | Royal Irish Constabulary, Silver | | £75 |
| jj | Scottish Police, Silver | | £75 |
| kk | St Andrew's Ambulance Corps, Silver | | £175 |
| ll | St John's Ambulance Corps, Silver | | £65 |
| mm | Royal Parks (109), Silver | | £180 |
| nn | Police Ambulance Service, Silver | | £300 |
| oo | **Visit to Ireland 1911** (2480), Silver | | £60 |
| pp | **Delhi Durbar 1911** | | |
| | 1 Gold (200) £675 | 2 Silver (30,000) | £40 |
| qq | **Jubilee 1935** | | |
| | (85,000), Silver | | £15 |

181 ee

181 cc (*reverse*)

181 cc

181 ff

181 gg

181 hh

181 ii

181 jj

181 kk

181 ll

181 mm

181 nn

181 oo

181 pp
(*reverse*)

181 qq

GEORGE VI

rr **Coronation 1937** (90,280), Silver £15

181 rr

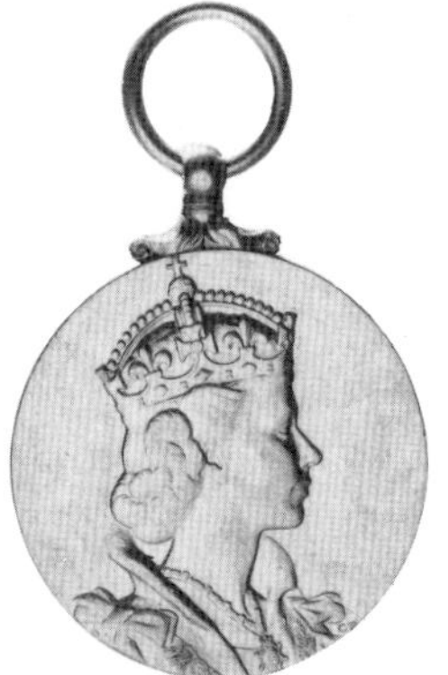
181 ss

181 tt (2)

181 tt (1)

ELIZABETH II

ss **Coronation 1953**
1 Silver (129,050) £20
2 impressed to 1953 Mount Everest team, Silver £250

tt **Jubilee 1977**
1 (30,000), Silver £95
2 Canadian issue, Silver £65

*Many of the numbers issued have been extracted from* Coronation and Royal Commemorative Medals 1887–1977 *by H. N. Cole to which readers should refer for a detailed study.*

## 182 Meritorious Service and Long Service Decorations and Medals

These awards were first introduced in 1830 by the Army and a year later by the Navy, followed rather later on by very many other units in the UK and in the Commonwealth, such as the Militia, Volunteers, Imperial Yeomanry, Naval Volunteers, etc. The end result is that there are a very great variety of issues, many of which were awarded with different royal effigies and cyphers, which has enabled this series by itself to be an extremely interesting one for the younger collector, especially as very many of the medals are available for a comparatively small outlay.

Prior to 1830, there were no Long Service Medals as such, but commanding officers of regiments frequently awarded privately engraved medals for long and meritorious service generally, and many were extremely well executed which today command fairly high prices. The whole series of official medals is mentioned in a fairly casual way by several older reference books but, in more recent times, a selection of the medals has been the subject of an exhaustive study by J. M. A. Tamplin, published by Spink & Son Ltd.

## 182 Meritorious Service Medals

182 c

a **Royal Navy**

| | | |
|---|---|---|
| 1 | George V (1919–28) | £200 |
| 2 | E.IIR. (1977) | £250 |

b **Royal Marines**

| | | | | | |
|---|---|---|---|---|---|
| 1 | Victoria (with '1848' below bust) | £425 | 4 | George V | £65 |
| 2 | Victoria | £125 | 5 | George VI | £65 |
| 3 | Edward VII | £85 | 6 | E.IIR. | £95 |

c **Army**

| | | | | | |
|---|---|---|---|---|---|
| 1 | Victoria (edge dated) | £350 | 7 | George VI (coinage head), with or without 'Ind.Imp' | £40 |
| 2 | Victoria (with '1848' below bust) | £425 | 8 | George VI (crowned head) | £150 |
| 3 | Victoria | £125 | 9 | E.IIR. (both issues) | £120 |
| 4 | Edward VII | £80 | | | |
| 5 | George V ('special' award, normally given) for wartime services | £60 | | | |
| 6 | George VI (coinage head) | £40 | | | |

d **Royal Air Force**

| | | | | | |
|---|---|---|---|---|---|
| 1 | George V | £145 | 2 | E.IIR. | £185 |

e **Australia**

| | | | | | |
|---|---|---|---|---|---|
| 1 | Edward VII | £475 | 3 | George VI | £100 |
| 2 | George V | £150 | 4 | E.IIR. | £70 |

f **Indian Army**

| | | | | | |
|---|---|---|---|---|---|
| 1 | Victoria (HEIC arms obverse) | £250 | 4 | George V ('Kaiser-i-Hind' legend) | £45 |
| 2 | Victoria (lotus wreath reverse) | £50 | 5 | George V ('Ind.Imp' legend) | £55 |
| 3 | Edward VII | £50 | 6 | George VI | £30 |

g **Colonial Police**

| | | |
|---|---|---|
| 1 | George VI | £125 |
| 2 | E.IIR. | £150 |

h **African Police**

| | | |
|---|---|---|
| 1 | George V | £200 |
| 2 | George VI | £250 |

i **South African Police**

| | | |
|---|---|---|
| 1 | George V | £125 |
| 2 | George VI | £150 |

j **South African Permanent Forces 1929–39**

| | | |
|---|---|---|
| 1 | George V | £140 |
| 2 | George VI | £225 |

182 f

LONG SERVICE AND GOOD CONDUCT MEDALS

## 183 The Royal Household

**The Faithful Service Medal**

| | | |
|---|---|---|
| a | Victoria | £300 |
| b | Edward VII | £450 |
| c | George V | £200 |
| d | George VI | £200 |
| e | E.IIR. | £175 |
| f | with 1 bar added | £225 |
| g | with 2 bars added | £300 |

183 f

## 184 Navy

a **Royal Navy—Medal**

| | | |
|---|---|---|
| 1 | William IV, anchor reverse (644) | £550 |
| 2 | Victoria, 1.5in suspender 8in '1848' below bust (100) | £700 |
| 3 | Victoria, 1.5in suspender (3572) | £150 |
| 4 | Victoria, 1.25in suspender with engraved naming (4400) | £65 |
| 5 | Victoria, 1.25in suspender with impressed naming (18,200) | £40 |
| 6 | Edward VII | £30 |
| 7 | George V, Admiral's bust, 1st issue | £25 |
| 8 | George V, coinage head, 2nd issue | £30 |
| 9 | George VI | £30 |
| 10 | George VI, without 'Ind.Imp' legend | £45 |
| 11 | E.IIR., fixed suspender, 1st issue | £50 |
| 12 | E.IIR., swivel suspender, 2nd issue | £40 |

*Numbers issued, in brackets, kindly supplied by Captain K. J. Douglas-Morris, RN*

b **The Royal Naval Reserve Decoration**

| | | |
|---|---|---|
| 1 | Edward VII | £110 |
| 2 | George V | £80 |
| 3 | George VI | £80 |
| 4 | E.IIR. | £95 |

c **The Royal Naval Reserve Medal**

| | | |
|---|---|---|
| 1 | Edward VII | £25 |
| 2 | George V, Admiral's bust, 1st issue | £25 |
| 3 | George V, coinage head, 2nd issue | £20 |
| 4 | George VI, 'Ind.Imp' legend, 1st issue | £30 |
| 5 | George VI, excluding 'Ind.Imp' legend, 2nd issue | £30 |
| 6 | E.IIR., fixed suspender, 1st issue | £50 |
| 7 | E.IIR., swivel suspender, 2nd issue | £35 |

184 c

d **The Royal Naval Volunteer Reserve Decoration**

1 Edward VII £185
2 George V £80
3 George VI, 'G.R.I' cypher, 1st issue £80
4 George VI, 'G.VIR.' cypher, 2nd issue £100
5 E.IIR. £100

e **The Royal Naval Volunteer Reserve Medal**

1 Edward VII £250
2 George V, Admiral's bust, 1st issue £65
3 George V, coinage head, 2nd issue £85
4 George VI, 'Ind. Imp' legend, 2nd issue £75
5 George VI, excluding 'Ind. Imp' legend, 2nd issue £85
6 E.IIR. £65

f **The Royal Fleet Reserve Medal**

1 George V, Admiral's bust, 1st issue £25
2 George V, coinage head, 2nd issue £20
3 George VI, 'Ind.Imp' legend, 1st issue £30
4 George VI, excluding 'Ind. Imp' legend, 2nd issue £30
5 E.IIR., 'Brit. Omn' legend, 1st issue £50
6 E.IIR., excluding 'Brit. Omn' legend, 2nd issue £35

g **The Royal Naval and Royal Naval Volunteer Reserve Auxiliary Sick Berth Medal**

1 George V, Admiral's bust, 1st issue £110
2 George V, coinage head, 2nd issue £120
3 George VI £75

h **The Royal Naval Wireless Auxiliary Reserve Medal**

1 George V, Admiral's bust, 1st issue £150
2 George V, coinage head, 2nd issue £175
3 George VI £140

i **The Royal Naval Auxiliary Services Medal**
E.IIR. £120

j **The Coastguard Auxiliary Service Medal**
E.IIR. £100

k **The Rocket Apparatus Volunteer Medal**
1 George V £40
2 George VI, 'Ind.Imp' legend, 1st issue £45
3 George VI, excluding 'Ind.Imp' legend, 2nd issue £70
4 E.IIR., 'Brit.Omn' legend, 1st issue £70
5 E.IIR., excluding 'Brit. Omn' legend, 2nd issue £60

l **The Royal Naval Dockyard Police—Hong Kong**
1 George V £110
2 George VI, 'Ind.Imp' legend, 1st issue £100
3 George VI, excluding 'Ind. Imp' legend, 2nd issue £135

184 i 184 a (*reverse*) 184 k (*reverse*) 184 k

## 185 Regular Army

a **Regular Army**

| | | |
|---|---|---|
| 1 | William IV, shield of Hanover in obverse centre | £425 |
| 2 | Victoria, steel clip and ring, rim dated, 1st issue | £120 |
| 3 | Victoria, scroll suspender, large reverse letters, 2nd issue | £80 |
| 4 | Victoria, scroll suspender, smaller reverse letters, 3rd issue | £35 |
| 5 | Edward VII | £25 |
| 6 | George V, swivel suspender, 1st issue 1911–20 | £20 |
| 7 | George V, fixed suspender, 2nd issue 1920–30 | £25 |
| 8 | George V, 'Regular Army' suspender, 3rd issue | £35 |
| 9 | George V, with a Commonwealth bar | £80 |
| 10 | George VI, either type | £25 |
| 11 | George VI, with a Commonwealth bar | £80 |
| 12 | E.IIR., either type | £30 |
| 13 | E.IIR., with a Commonwealth bar | £85 |

## 186 Volunteer, Territorial and Efficiency Decorations and Medals

b **The Volunteer Decoration**

| | | |
|---|---|---|
| 1 | Victoria, 'VR' cypher | £50 |
| 2 | Victoria, 'VRI' cypher | £150 |
| 3 | Edward VII | £85 |

185 a (4)

185 a (2)

185 a (8)

c **The Efficiency Decoration**

| | | |
|---|---|---|
| 1 | George V, 'Territorial' suspender | £50 |
| 2 | George V, 'India' suspender | £70 |
| 3 | George VI, 'GRI' cypher with 'Territorial' suspender | £45 |
| 4 | George VI, 'GRI' cypher with 'India' suspender | £65 |
| 5 | George VI, 'GRVI' cypher with 'Territorial' suspender | £60 |
| 6 | George VI, 'GRVI' cypher | £50 |
| 7 | E.IIR., with 'Territorial' suspender | £60 |
| 8 | E.IIR., with 'A.E.R.' suspender | £90 |
| 9 | E.IIR., with 'T&A.V.R.' suspender | £90 |
| 10 | Any of the above with a Commonwealth bar (not India, A.E.R. or T & A.V.R.) | from £90 |

d **The Territorial Decoration**

| | | |
|---|---|---|
| 1 | Edward VII | £70 |
| 2 | George V | £40 |

186 b (1)

186 d (2)

186 f (1)

e **The Territorial Force Efficiency Medal**

| | |
|---|---|
| 1 Edward VII | £30 |
| 2 George V (with 'Territorial Force' or 'Territorial' reverse) | £20 |

f **The Efficiency Medal**

| | |
|---|---|
| 1 George V, 'Territorial' suspender | £30 |
| 2 George V, 'Militia' suspender | £70 |
| 3 George V, 'India' suspender | £50 |
| 4 George VI, 'Territorial' suspender | £35 |
| 5 George VI, Territorial suspender but without 'Ind.Imp' legend | £50 |
| 6 George VI, 'Militia' suspender | £80 |
| 7 George VI, 'Militia' suspender but without 'Ind.Imp' legend | £90 |
| 8 George VI, 'India' suspender | £60 |
| 9 George VI, 'Army Emergency Reserve' suspender | £140 |
| 10 E.IIR., 'Territorial' suspender (both legends) | £50 |
| 11 E.IIR., 'Army Emergency Reserve' suspender (both legends) | £140 |
| 12 E.IIR., 'Militia' suspender | £125 |
| 13 E.IIR. 'T&A.V.R.' suspender | £100 |
| 14 Any of the above with a Commonwealth bar (not India, A.E.R Militia or T & A.V.R.) | from £60 |

186 f (3)

186 h

MISCELLANEOUS

g **Ulster Defence Regiment**

| | |
|---|---|
| 1 Long Service and Good Conduct Medal (Permanent Service) 1970 E.IIR. | £150 |
| 2 Regimental Medal (Part-time) 1970 E.IIR. | £150 |

h **The Militia Medal**

| | |
|---|---|
| 1 Edward VII | £85 |
| 2 George V | £140 |

186 i

186 j

186 k (3–7)

| | | |
|---|---|---|
| i | **The Imperial Yeomanry Medal** | |
| | Edward VII | £130 |
| j | **The Special Reserve Medal** | |
| | 1 Edward VII | £125 |
| | 2 George V | £100 |
| k | **The Indian Army Long Service Medal** | |
| | 1 Victoria, HEIC arms, 1848 issue | £375 |
| | 2 Victoria, anchor reverse, 1859 issue | £450 |
| | 3 Victoria, lotus wreath reverse, 1888 issue | £40 |
| | 4 Edward VII | £35 |
| | 5 George V, 'Kaiser-i-Hind' obverse, 1st issue | £25 |
| | 6 George V, without 'Kaiser-i-Hind', 2nd issue | £30 |
| | 7 George VI | £25 |
| l | **The Indian Volunteer Decoration** | |
| | 1 Edward VII | £150 |
| | 2 George V | £80 |
| m | **The Volunteer Force Long Service Medal** | |
| | 1 Victoria, 'Vic.Reg.' obverse, UK issue | £35 |
| | 2 Victoria, 'Vic.Reg.et Imp' obverse, overseas issue | £60 |
| | 3 Edward VII, 'Rex Imp' obverse, UK recipients | £50 |
| | 4 Edward VII, 'Rex Imp' obverse, overseas recipients | £70 |
| | 5 Edward VII, 'Kaiser-i-Hind' obverse, Indian issue | £30 |
| | 6 George V | £85 |
| n | **The Permanent Forces of the Empire Beyond the Seas Medal** | |
| | 1 Edward VII | £250 |
| | 2 George V | £125 |

*Based on medals to Canadian units*

186 l (2)　　186 m

186 o (3)

o **The Colonial Auxiliary Forces Decoration**

| | | |
|---|---|---|
| 1 | Victoria | £200 |
| 2 | Edward VII | £145 |
| 3 | George V | £90 |

p **The Colonial Auxiliary Forces Medal**

| | | |
|---|---|---|
| 1 | Victoria | £120 |
| 2 | Edward VII | £90 |
| 3 | George V | £80 |

q **The Canadian Forces Decoration**

| | | | | | |
|---|---|---|---|---|---|
| 1 | George VI | £65 | 3 | E.IIR., with 1 bar | £50 |
| 2 | E.IIR. | £35 | 4 | E.IIR., with 2 bars | £90 |

r **The Canadian Long Service Medal**

| | | |
|---|---|---|
| 1 | Victoria | £200 |
| 2 | Edward VII | £200 |

s **The New Zealand Long Service Medal**

| | | |
|---|---|---|
| 1 | Victoria | £175 |
| 2 | Edward VII | £175 |

ss **The New Zealand Territorial Service Medal**

| | |
|---|---|
| George V | £125 |

t **The Cape of Good Hope Long Service Medal**

| | | |
|---|---|---|
| 1 | Victoria | £98 |
| 2 | Edward VII | £38 |

u **The Royal West African Frontier Force and King's African Rifles Long Service Medals**

| | | |
|---|---|---|
| 1 | Edward VII | £125 |
| 2 | George V | £85 |
| 3 | George VI | £100 |

186 p

186 q (2)

186 ss

v **South African Permanent Forces Long Service Medal**
1 George VI, with 'Ind.Imp' obverse, 2nd issue £150
2 George VI, without 'Ind.Imp' obverse, 2nd issue £300

w **The Cadet Forces Medal**
1 George VI £60
2 E.IIR. £45

x **The Royal Observer Corps Medal**
1 George VI £90
2 E.IIR. £60

y **The Civil Defence Medal**
1 E.IIR. £30
2 E.IIR. Ulster issue 'CD:A.F.R.S:H.S.R.' reverse £95

z **The Women's Voluntary Services Medal** £20

aa **The Voluntary Medical Services Medal**
1 Silver £30
2 Cupro-nickel £12

bb **The St John's Ambulance Brigade Medal**
1 Silver £30
2 Base metal £12

cc **The Queen Alexandra's Imperial Nursing Service Reserve**
1 Edward VII £35 2 George V £30

186 y (2)
186 aa
186 bb
187 a

## 187 Police Forces

a **Police** (UK issue)

| | | |
|---|---|---|
| 1 | George VI | £20 |
| 2 | E.IIR. | £20 |

b **Special Constabulary**

| | | |
|---|---|---|
| 1 | George V (both issues) | £5 |
| 2 | George VI | £5 |
| 3 | George VI, without 'Ind.Imp' | £25 |
| 4 | E.IIR. | £10 |

c **Special Constabulary, Ulster**
E.IIR. £110

d **Special Constabulary, Colonial**
E.IIR. £145

e **The Colonial Police Medal**
1 George V £120
2 George VI (both issues) £80
3 E.IIR. (both issues) £95

f **The Cyprus Military Police Medal**
George V £350

g **The Ceylon Police Medal**
George V £175

h **The Malta Police Medal**
1 George V, crowned head £300
2 George V, coinage head £450

i **The South African Police Medal**
All three issues £45

## 188 Fire Brigades

a **The Fire Brigades Medal** (UK issue)
E.IIR. £65

b **The Colonial Fire Brigade Medal**
1 George V £400
2 George VI £300
3 E.IIR. £300

187 b (1–4, *reverse*)

## 189 Prisons Service

a **Colonial Prisons Service**
E.IIR. (both issues) £190

b **South African Prisons Service** £90

190 a
(*reverse*)

## 190 Royal Air force

a **The Long Service Medal**

| | | |
|---|---|---|
| 1 | George V | £70 |
| 2 | George VI | £50 |
| 3 | George VI with 'RAF Levies Iraq' suspender | £400 |
| 4 | E.IIR. | £40 |

b **The Air Efficiency Medal**

| | | |
|---|---|---|
| 1 | George VI (both issues) | £60 |
| 2 | E.IIR. (both issues) | £100 |

## Medals for Life-Saving, etc

Prior to the institution of the Government's first official life-saving medal, namely the Albert Medal in 1877, the only awards were those sparingly presented by the various life-saving societies from as far back as the latter part of the eighteenth century. These private awards are often keenly sought after by collectors, with many of the citations being available, Many of the principal awards are listed below, but a detailed study will shortly be available; it will be the first specialized publication covering this subject, entitled *Unofficial Lifesaving Awards* by W. Fevyer.

## 191 Royal National Lifeboat Institution

| | | 1 Gold | 2 Silver | 3 Bronze |
|---|---|---|---|---|
| a | George IV | £900 | £220 | —— |
| b | Victorian | £900 | £220 | —— |
| c | Edward VII | £1500 | £300 | —— |
| d | George V | £1000 | £250 | £150 |
| e | Sir William Hillary issues | £1100 | £180 | £100 |

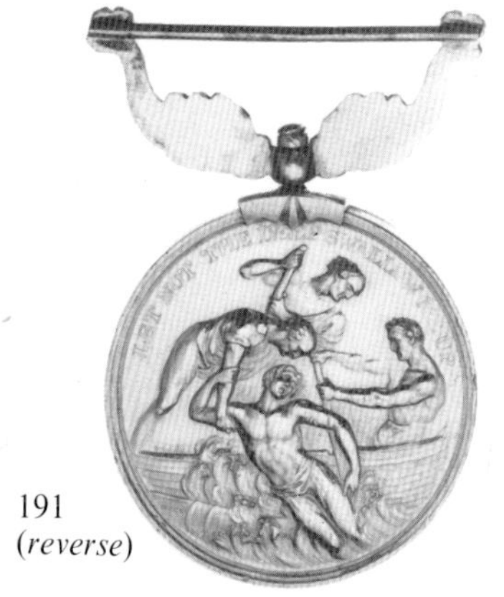

191
(*reverse*)

191b

191 e

## 192 Liverpool Shipwreck & Humane Society

| | | 1 Gold | 2 Silver | 3 Bronze |
|---|---|---|---|---|
| a | Marine Medal, 1st Type (medallion) | £1500 | £150 | —— |
| b | Marine Medal, 2nd type (oval) | —— | £250 | —— |
| c | Marine Medal, 3rd type (medal) | £800 | £45 | £25 |
| d | Fire Medal | £1500 | £160 | £60 |
| e | General issue | £1300 | £60 | £35 |
| f | Camp & Villaverde Medal | —— | £375 | £150 |
| g | Bramley-Moore Medal | £2000 | £350 | £140 |
| h | Memoriam Medallion | —— | £200 | £130 |

192

192

## 193 Shipwrecked Fishermen & Mariners Royal Benevolent Society

1 Gold £800 2 Silver £125

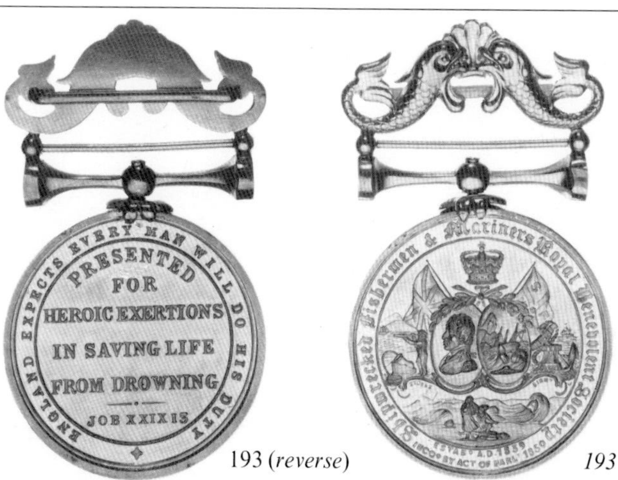

193 (*reverse*) *193*

## 194 The C.Q.D. (S.O.S.) Medal

£65

194 (*reverse*) 194

## 195 St John's Life Saving

| 1 Gold £950 | 2 Silver £125 | 3 Bronze £65 |
|---|---|---|

195

195

196 196 (*reverse*) 197a

## 196 Royal Society Protection of Life from Fire

| 1 | Silver | £120 | 2 | Bronze | £60 |
|---|---|---|---|---|---|

197 b (*reverse*) 197 b

## 197 Royal Humane Society Medals

| | | 1 Silver | 2 Bronze |
|---|---|---|---|
| a | Early large 2in dia. | £150 | £60 |
| b | Later 1.5in worn from a riband | £125 | £40 |

*Prices apply to both the successful and unsuccessful issues*

## 198 Royal Humane Society's Stanhope Gold Medal

| | |
|---|---|
| | £1500 |

*See Nos 56 and 57 for the official British Government issues, ie the Sea Gallantry Medal and the Sea Gallantry Medal (Foreign Services)*

## 199 Lloyd's Medal for Saving Life at Sea

| | | | | | |
|---|---|---|---|---|---|
| 1 | Silver | £250 | 2 | Bronze | £125 |

199
(*reverse*)

199

## 200 Lloyd's Medal for Meritorious Services

| | |
|---|---|
| | £300 |

## 201 Lloyd's Medal for Services to Lloyd's

| | |
|---|---|
| | £250 |

## 202 Lloyd's War Medal for Bravery at Sea

| | |
|---|---|
| | £450 |

## 203 Hundred of Salford

£95

## 204 Hartley Colliery

£225

204

206

## 205 Drummond Castle

(silver) £200

## 206 SS *Titanic*/RMS *Carpathia* 1912

| 1 Gold £1750 | 2 Silver £150 | 3 Bronze £90 |
|---|---|---|

# REFERENCE BOOKS

Reference books are the life-blood of any serious collector. Medal collectors are fortunate that histories and historically-based books will often provide information regarding a medal or a campaign in a general way.

For the specialist collector there are a number of books available. Listed below are recommended titles—both new and second-hand—that can be obtained through bookshops, or from Spink & Son Ltd.

*(Prices correct at time of going to press).*

DORLING, H. TAPRELL, *Ribbons and Medals*. New edition 1983. Edited and revised by Alec A. Purves. 500+ pages, over 500 photographs, £20

FEVYER, W.H. *The George Medal (1940-1945)*. 1980, 114 pages, 2 plates. Laminated card covers, £9.50

FEVYER, W.H. *The Distinguished Service Medal, 1939-1946*. 1981, 163 pages, 1 plate. Cloth, £20

FEVYER, W.H. *The Queen's South Africa Medal Roll 1983,* 156 pages, £20

JACOB, J.R. *Court Jewellers of the World*. 1978, 92 pages, plates, many of Stars of Orders. Cloth, £12.50

JOSLIN, E.C. (Revisor). *British Battles and Medals*, by Major L.L. Gordon. Fifth revised edition, 1979. 437 pages, plates. Cloth, £16

JOSLIN, E.C. *The Observer's Book of British Awards and Medals,* 1974. 192 pages, illustrations. Cloth, £1.95

POULSOM, Major. N.W. *The White Ribbon*: A medallic record of British Polar Expeditions. 1968. 215 pages, 9 plates, maps. Cloth, £5

RISK, J.C. *The History of the Order of the Bath and its Insignia*. 1972, 150 pages, 26 plates, some in colour. Frontispiece of H.M. Queen Elizabeth II in full colour. Cloth, £8

RISK, J.C. *British Orders and Decorations*. London 1973, 124 pages, 76 plates and frontispiece. Cloth, £2

STONE, A.G. *Indian Campaigns 1778-1914*. 17 pages. Reprinted from the Numismatic Circular. 1974. Card covers, £1

TAMPLIN, J.M.A. *The Imperial Yeomanry Long Service and Good Conduct Medal*. 1978. (Spink Medal Booklet, No. 1). 52 pages. Card covers, £3

TAMPLIN, J.M.A. *The Militia Long Service and Good Conduct Medal*. (Spink Medal Booklet No. 2). 52 pages. Card covers, £4

TAMPLIN, J.M.A. *The Special Reserve Long Service and Good Conduct Medal*. (Spink Medal Booklet, No. 3). 40 pages. Card covers, £4.50

TAMPLIN, J.M.A. *The Volunteer Officers' Decoration*. 1980. (Spink Medal Booklet No. 4). 48 pages, 16 illustrations. Card covers, £4.50

TAMPLIN, J.M.A. *Volunteer Long Service Medals*. 1981. (Spink Medal Booklet No. 5). 48 pages, 10 illustrations. Card covers, £5.50

TAMPLIN, J.M.A. *The Colonial Auxiliary Forces Officers' Decoration. The Indian Volunteer Forces Officers' Decoration*. 1981. (Spink Medal Booklet No. 6). 88 pages, 13 illustrations. Card covers, £7.50

TINSON, Major A.R. *Orders, Decorations and Medals of the Sultanate of Oman*. Published for the Government of Oman, 1978. 112 pages, 15 colour plates. Cloth, £14

***A catalogue of books which are currently available is obtainable from Spink & Son Ltd.***

A SELECTION OF OUT OF PRINT WORKS SOMETIMES AVAILABLE FROM STOCK.

MAYO, J.H. *Medals and Decorations of the British Army and Navy*. 1897. 2 volumes (88), 617 pages, 56 plates, figures in the text.

SPINK & SON. *The War Medal Record, including Orders of Knighthood.* London 1896-1898. 2 volumes (24) (11), 479 pages, plates, figures in the text.

TANCRED, G. *Historical Record of Medals and Honorary Distinctions conferred on the British Navy, Army and Auxiliary Forces. 1891. (16) 483 pages, 24 plates.*

*CREAGH, Sir O'Moore and HUMPHRIS, E.M. The V.C. and D.S.O. London*. 1924, 3 volumes: I *The V.C.* 355 pages, 722 portraits. II *The D.S.O.* 452 pages, 713 portraits. III *The D.S.O.* (continued) 381 pages, 313 portraits. Biographical details of recipients of the awards up to the date of publication.

# The Design and Manufacturing of ORDERS, DECORATIONS and SERVICE MEDALS

For almost 100 years Spink's medal department has built up expertise and experience in this particular field which today is second to none.

In recent years they have individually designed and manufactured, in their own London factory, Orders and Medals for a very considerable number of countries.

Their general experience and extensive historical knowledge of the World's decorations, places them in an unrivalled position not only to design and manufacture, but also of equal importance, to advise and guide Governments, as an after-sales service, which system they should adopt so as to administer effectively the distribution and recording of such awards.

Also very important is the advice and guidance we can render Governments when the question of introducing decora tions for the first time is considered. This ensures from the outset that any system of awards adopted will be introduced in accordance with normal international practice, taking into account local requirements.

Governments are invited to send us, in the first instance, an outline of their requirements, with, if possible, some rough sketches. We will then submit for approval our artist's preliminary colour sketches, which, after consideration, can then be resubmitted in the form of fine finished designs.

Decorations and Medals have for many centuries, been awarded as a means of visually recognising meritorious service. Even in modern times they are still the only practical means of a country conveying its appreciation for exceptional services.

Individually designed awards created for:

The Armed Forces
The Police
National Fire Brigades
The Prison Services
Government Employees
Civilians
Foreigners
The Diplomatic Corps

A selection of countries for which Spink have created and produced Orders, Decorations and Medals:

Abu Dhabi
Aden
Alberta
Bahamas
Bahrain
Bermuda
Bhutan
Botswana
Brazil
Brunei
Burma
Canada
Czechoslovakia
Dubai
Ethiopia
France
Gambia
Ghana
Greece
Guyana
Holland
Indian Princely States
Iraq
Jamaica
Kedah
Kenya
Kuwait
Lesotho
Libya
Luxembourg
Malawi
Malta
Muscat
Negri Sembilan
New Zealand
Nigeria
Norway
Oman
Pahang
Pakistan
Poland
Qatar
Ras al Khaimah
Roumania
Sarawak
Sabah
Selangor
Sierra Leone
Singapore
Sikkim
Solomon Islands
Sudan
Tanzania
Uganda
United Arab Emirates
United Kingdom

# Index

**Dated Stars and Bars**